Food Prints

An Epicurean Voyage through Pakistan:
Overview of Pakistani Cuisine

Food Prints

An Epicurean Voyage through Pakistan:
Overview of Pakistani Cuisine

Shanaz Ramzi

OXFORD

UNIVERSITY PRESS

Oxford University Press is a department of the University of Oxford.
It furthers the University's objective of excellence in research, scholarship,
and education by publishing worldwide in

Oxford New York

Auckland Cape Town Dar es Salaam Hong Kong Karachi
Kuala Lumpur Madrid Melbourne Mexico City Nairobi
New Delhi Shanghai Taipei Toronto

With offices in

Argentina Austria Brazil Chile Czech Republic France Greece
Guatemala Hungary Italy Japan Poland Portugal Singapore
South Korea Switzerland Turkey Ukraine Vietnam

Oxford is a registered trademark of Oxford University Press
in the UK and in certain other countries

Published in Pakistan by Oxford University Press

ISBN 978-0-19-906325-3

Photography Credits

Introduction: p. xii, p. xiii, p. xv Muhammad Rizwan.
Chapter 1: p. 4 Rehan Zaheer; p. 6 Jawaid Islam; p. 7 Shahid Hussain;
p. 8 Batool Nasir; p. 11 Ather Syed. **Chapter 3:** p. 22 Batool Nasir.
Chapter 6: p. 50 Imran Schah. **Chapter 8:** p. 90 Danial Shah.
Chapter 9: p. 98 Raja Islam; p. 103 Shahid Hussain.
Chapter 10: p. 108 Batool Nasir

Typeset in Goudy Old Style, Harrington
Printed in Malaysia
Published by
Ameena Saiyid, Oxford University Press
No. 38, Sector 15, Korangi Industrial Area, PO Box 8214,
Karachi-74900, Pakistan.

To my husband who has stoically put up with all the hours I
have spent these past seven years researching for, and writing the book

In loving memory of my parents

Contents

Acknowledgements

The seeds for writing a book on Pakistan's varied cuisine were sown when Oxford University Press (OUP) requested that I write a book for their children's series on Pakistani cuisine, a few years ago. After I had sent them the first draft, and it had been approved, there was a change in their policy with regard to pictorial books, with the result that all such ventures in the pipeline, including mine, were scrapped. Since my 'grey cells' had already gone into over-drive, I decided I would not waste the opportunity that had knocked at my door, and would write the book anyway, but for adults. As it turns out, my book has done a full 360 degrees, for on learning about it Ameena Saiyid, Managing Director, OUP expressed an interest in seeing the manuscript, and decided to take it up! All I can say is I am deeply indebted to her and am thrilled it is back with OUP.

There is one person I need to acknowledge in particular—artist and activist, Jimmy Engineer—whose encouragement, and insistence on my writing a book was probably as instrumental in my finally getting down to doing it, as the opportunity provided by OUP. Thank you Jimmy for your faith in me. The other person who has been most encouraging is Yasmeen Lari. She has been witness to my long and arduous struggle researching for the book, and has been prodding me on to complete it.

One individual, without whose guidance and suggestions this book would have certainly been completed a lot earlier, but it would have lacked much of the depth, detailing and perspective it has today, is Mr Hamid Haroon. I am sincerely indebted to him for taking out time and providing his valuable suggestions and for setting me back by a good few months in the process!

I would also like to mention here three young individuals who have helped at different stages of the book. One is Shaziah Zuberi, who six years ago, voluntarily went around interviewing people to gather information for me, and the others are Iftikhar Hasan—Ifti, to my family—and Taha Shuja Hyder who have been responsible for the beautiful photographs of Pakistani cuisine you see in these pages. It would be remiss of me not to thank the management of Bar-B-Q Tonight here, for they went out of their way to facilitate these young photographers in getting some wonderful shots. Thanks also go out to the management of Rangoli restaurant for allowing photography of their cuisine. I would also like to express my heartfelt gratitude to the Pakistani cooking television channel *Masala* for the loan of some of their chefs' recipes and photographs of their cuisine.

Through these seven years I have taxed the brain of many an individual to glean an insight into the culinary specialties of their community, and would in particular, like to thank Raasta Development Consultants, Begum Gohar Sultan Gurchani (late), Faryal Gohar, Ruby and Neelam Habib, Javed and Yasmeen Iqbal, Mahtab Rashdi, Mumtaz Rashdi (late), Ather Viqar Azeem, Rabya Arif, Zahid Khan, Amna Moton, Rukhsana Esbahani, Dr Afshan Jafri, Afroza Bhamani, Mariam Halai, Amna Sarwar, Sehar Zaman, Birgul Bangash, Safia Muzaffer (late), Saba Shahid, Renu Perwani, Dr Ruqayya Saeed Hashmi, Syed Zaheer-ul-Islam, Naima Shamsi, Nasreen Dossani, Farzana Ali, Bilkis Qureshi, Daulat Rahimtoola, Ayesha Ahmed, Khwaja Farooq Ahmed, and Salma Chundrigar for their valuable input.

I must thank Mr Asif Noorani, who I look upon as my mentor, for taking out his valuable time to edit the book informally at its initial stage and then again at its final stage. I am also indebted to Anwer Mooraj for going through the entire manuscript and giving his candid opinions and suggestions regarding the text, and particularly for his very pertinent advice, which I followed, of adding recipes in the book.

Finally, it goes without saying that none of this would have been possible if God had not supported me all the way. The book is just one more of the many things I remain eternally grateful to Him for.

Preface

This book strives to document the influence of geography, history, culture and religion on the culinary habits of Pakistan. While acquiring a general idea about the kind of fare that forms the staple diet of the country, the reader will become acquainted with the many communities that now inhabit the various parts of Pakistan and the cuisines they enjoy in particular. They will also learn about the origins of many of the popular dishes, the enchanting legends behind some of them and the occasions they are most associated with.

However, there is a plethora of dishes patronised by the different communities living in Pakistan and I do realize that many may feel that this or that dish has been left out. All I can say is, I have tried my best to include all the major specialties of every community, but if I have inadvertently overlooked any dish, please do convey it to me and I shall try and add it in the next edition! So, fret not, and enjoy your epicurean voyage through Pakistan. *Bon appétit!*

Introduction

Imprints on Pakistan

Located to the north-west of India, just below the towering snowcapped Himalayas and above the warm waters of the Arabian Sea; with Afghanistan, China and Iran as its immediate neighbours, Pakistan is a country greatly influenced by diverse cultures. In fact, Pakistan has been rightly described as standing at the crossroads of the world where the cultures of the Middle East and Asia meet and become one. Physically a dramatic country, its very varied topography has also played an important role in giving birth to a kaleidoscope of customs, norms and cuisines that few countries can boast of. Pakistan is home to eight of the ten highest peaks of the world, as well as gigantic melting glaciers, which feed the mighty River Indus, winding its way through the country for over 2800 kilometres. The long and meandering ribbon of river separates beautiful valleys and rich and fertile plains from barren deserts that are as much a part of Pakistan's terrain as its fertile plains and mountains.

And its history is as rich as they come. Although Pakistan may only be 64 years old, born out of the ashes of Imperial India, it has inherited the beauty of its ancient past that dates back to two of the oldest societies of the world: Mehrgarh—which existed from perhaps the sixth millennium in present-day Balochistan, and where wheat and barley agriculture was practised (Sharif and Thapar 1992/1999)—and the Indus Valley where a highly civilized society existed around 2600–1900 BC (Papiha, Deka, and Chakraborty 1999). With its cities blossoming even before Babylon came into existence, its people practised the art of good living and citizenship—including planned urban developments and the use of a still un-deciphered script, standardized weights, and craft technologies—long before the celebrated ancient Greeks (Kenoyer 2010; Possehl 2002; Gidwani 2006).

Pakistan's chequered history is a saga of invasions beginning with the wild, barbaric nomads from central Asia, known as the Aryans, who some historians believe conquered the people of the Indus Valley around 1500 BC and settled in the Sapta Sindhu (Seven Rivers) the region round about the Sindhu (Indus) and other rivers, till 600 BC (Garg 1992). They developed a pastoral society that grew into the Rigvedic Civilization. The Veda—texts associated with the complex ritual system of the Aryans—is believed to have been composed in this period (Chatterjee 1998), and form one important basis for the religion we now call 'Hinduism'.

Sharing some of the basic assumptions of developing Hindu thought, Buddha began his teachings in the sixth century BC. It was towards the end of the sixth century too, that Darius I of Iran organized Sindh and the Punjab as the twentieth satrapy of his empire. The Greek armies of Alexander the Great of Macedonia appeared in the fourth century BC, defeating Darius III in 331 BC (Lari 2000). Buddhism gained ground, particularly in what is now known as northern Punjab, during the reign of the Mauryan dynasty (323–185 BC). Bactrian Greeks re-established Greek rule in Pakistan in 185 BC.

In the second century AD, the Kushans, a group of nomadic warriors from central Asia, conquered the Gandharan region of northern Pakistan. Then, in early eighth century AD, Mohammed Bin Qasim arrived, heralding Arab rule in the lower half of Pakistan for two hundred years. It was during this time that Islam took roots in the soil and greatly influenced the life, culture, cuisine and traditions of the people.

Since the twelfth century the rulers of the Delhi Sultanate—a succession of various Turkish, Afghan, Persian and Central Asian dynasties who ruled from their capital in Delhi for more than 300 years (Sen 2004)—had begun to leave their mark on the cuisine of the country. In AD 1498, the first Europeans arrived when the Portuguese explorer Vasco de Gama opened up the sea route to the Indies (Collingham 2006), introducing ingredients and recipes that were alien to the country. The glorious reign of the Mughal dynasty (from AD 1526), founded by Babar, a Turkish/Central Asian chieftain whose ancestors included the Mongol leader, Changez Khan, and Timur (known in the west as Tamerlane), also brought with it a rich gastronomy strongly influenced by Persian and Turkic cuisines, as well as those of Central Asia and Afghanistan. The Islamic imperial power ended in mid-nineteenth century, ultimately giving way to the British colonization of the subcontinent. When Pakistan came into being in 1947, it became home not only to the many communities already living in the areas that constituted Pakistan, but also to the many Muslims that had been settled in different parts of India who abandoned their motherland to make Pakistan their abode. What's more, to add to the potpourri of cultures already prevalent in the country there was an influx of refugees, first from Bangladesh then from Afghanistan, following Pakistan's birth.

Understandably, all these settlers have left their imprints on the country and, of course, its populace. Today, the 170 million or so people that make up the population of Pakistan reflect a rich and disparate heritage in their lifestyles, beliefs and traditions. And, most of all in their exotic, varied and amazing cuisine, for there is no doubt that invasions and colonialism substantially influence the way a nation eats.

1

A Look at Pakistan's Geography and Anthropology

Pakistan comprises Khyber Pakhtunkhwa (previously North-West Frontier Province), FATA (Federally Administered Tribal Areas), Gilgit-Baltistan (previously Northern Areas), Sindh, the Punjab and Balochistan. Although, officially Azad Kashmir does not fall under Pakistan, for the purpose of this book I have included Pakistan Administered Jammu and Kashmir as well. Each area is distinct not only for its geographical features but also for the communities dominating it, giving the region an individual flavour and colour. While one may find members of every community settled all over Pakistan, they tend to be found in greatest numbers in the areas adopted as homeland by their forefathers, thus influencing the cuisine of that particular region the most. Therefore, even if a community exists in many parts of Pakistan, its cuisine has been dealt with in the context of the province where they are to be found in largest numbers. It is interesting to note that while an area's gastronomy is determined by the communities living in it, the same communities may enjoy different cuisines depending on where they are settled, as geographical factors also influence their preferences.

   I must add that the communities focused here are not because of the dialect or language they speak—in fact some linguistic tribes have not been mentioned at all—but for the uniqueness of their cuisine.

Khyber Pakhtunkhwa

Situated in the northwest of Pakistan, bound by Afghanistan to the west and north; Azad Kashmir to the northeast; the Punjab to the southeast; and Balochistan to the southwest

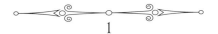

Kandahari Nan

lies Khyber Pakhtunkhwa. Dubbed as 'the land where the mountains meet'—both the ancient Silk and Spice routes run through it—this is a land of scenic beauty, the terrain of this province consisting of rugged mountain ranges, undulating hills and lush plains. In the north, the mountain ranges generally run north-south, and boast five river valleys running roughly parallel: Chitral, Dir, Swat, Indus and Kaghan. South of the Kabul River, which bisects the province from east to west, the ranges also generally run east-west. Khyber Pakhtunkhwa is accessible by land through natural mountain passes, the best known of which is the 56 kilometres long Khyber Pass. Since time immemorial the Pass has served as an entry-point to numerous invading armies and formed an important route for trade.

Khyber Pakhtunkhwa's economy is essentially agrarian, even though the largely mountainous terrain is not favourable to extensive cultivation. Irrigation is carried out on about one-third of the cultivated land and the principal crops grown are wheat, corn (maize), sugarcane and tobacco, while barley and millet are also harvested. Rice and spinach are also grown in the province. Fruits grown in abundance here, not to speak of dry fruits, are in great demand all over the country. Khyber Pakhtunkhwa, like Afghanistan, is notorious for its poppy crops.

A single community, the Pashtuns who are among the most numerous tribal people in the world—they account for over 15 per cent of the population of Pakistan, making them the second largest ethnic group in the country—predominantly inhabit Khyber Pakhtunkhwa. The racial composition of the Pashtuns (also known as Pakhtuns) is less than clear, to say the very least. By and large it is believed that the tribes which dwelt in the region, including Afghanistan, in the days of the Greek historians were part of the great Aryan migration from central Asia a millennium earlier, a belief that is given credence by the fact that their language is similar to that of the Aryans (Nijjar 2007). The Greek historian Herodotus also spoke of a group called the Pactyans living in the area around 1000 BC, while there is a description of the Pakthas in the region in the Rig-Veda. Some think that the Pashtuns may be related to the Bactrians, Scythians and/or Kushans. Still others suggest that they were first seen in the Kandahar area and could have been Jews, Zoroastrians, Buddhists or members of other religions prior to the Islamic invasion in the seventh century AD

Chapli Kebab, a Khyber Pakhtunkhwa specialty

(Nielson 2010). Over the course of centuries, inter-marriages with the Persian, Greek, Turk and Mongol invaders who passed through the frontier enriched their ethnic composition greatly.

While various divisions exist within the Pashtuns suffice it to say that the one trait that seems common to all the Pashtun tribes is that through the centuries they have managed to retain their cultural integrity. Their eating habits too, remain broadly the same, hence, the cuisine of the Pashtuns in general has been described under Khyber Pakhtunkhwa where they are to be found in the greatest numbers. A Pashtun community located to the south of Khyber Pakhtunkhwa that does need to be specifically singled out, though, exists basically in Bannu district—the Bannuchis. Ethnologically, the Bannuchis are believed to be Aryans with a mixture of Mongolian and Semitic blood (Latif 1975), and their cuisine is distinct.

A non-Pashtun community of Khyber Pakhtunkhwa that cannot be ignored is Hindkowans, an Indo-Aryan ethno-linguistic group native to Khyber Pakhtunkhwa but also found in substantial numbers in the Punjab and Kashmir. According to a survey conducted in 2008, they number nearly four million in Pakistan. Also, there are now anywhere between two million and five million Afghan refugees settled in Pakistan—census figures regarding their number are varied—with their greatest concentration in Khyber Pakhtunkhwa and FATA.

To the north of Khyber Pakhtunkhwa is the Chitral region, an area that supposedly boasts the greatest linguistic diversity in the world. The mountainous extreme north regions of the province are home to diverse ethnic groups that are nomadic in nature, generally referred to as Khow. The Khow are believed to be the backwash of the second wave of Aryan immigrants from about one millennium BC. Since then, hundreds of clans and tribes belonging to different ethnic groups have come to Chitral from the northern, southern, eastern and western passes, settled there and mingled with the Khow by intermarrying and adopting their culture. In later times, when Islam reached Chitral, all of them embraced the religion and became one people collectively called Khow or Khowistanis as they are now generally known (Aseer 2009). The main crop grown in Chitral is wheat followed by maize, rice, vegetables and fruit, and pulses on the arid land.

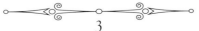

The lower part of Chitral was once home to the indigenous Kalash—meaning black, referring to the black clothing made of goat hair worn by their womenfolk—researched to be descendants of Alexander the Great's army, and now confined to three small valleys in Chitral—Bumburet, Rumbur and Birir. Numbering a few thousand, their way of life is rooted in the worship of ancestral spirits and trees, and they have managed to retain their unique culture and lifestyle. Two sets of crops are harvested in the Kalash villages—wheat as a winter crop, and maize, beans and vegetables as summer crops. Apples, grapes (generally used for wine which the Kalash are permitted to produce and drink), mulberry, pears, apricots, and walnuts are among the many foods grown in the area. Millet and barley used to be vital crops, but they seem to be vanishing (Bruun and Kalland 1995).

Close to the Khyber Pass, at the head of the fertile Indus Valley lies the verdant Peshawar, the capital of Khyber Pakhtunkhwa. Peshawar represents an urban city of Pakistan where people still closely adhere to their local customs and traditions. It is a city where residents have not incorporated changes in lifestyle at the same rate as residents of the larger cities of Pakistan, and consequently follow a slower pace of life. Interestingly enough, the largest urban population of Pashtuns is not concentrated in Peshawar but in Karachi. A number of Sikhs, on the other hand, are settled here, as in the tribal areas, though their largest concentration is in the Punjab.

FATA (Federally Administered Tribal Areas)

Comprising a region of some 27,220 square km FATA has Afghanistan to the north-west, Khyber Pakhtunkhwa to the east and Balochistan to the south. The seven districts known as agencies lying north to south that form FATA, are Bajaur, Mohmand, Khyber, Orakzai, Kurram, North Waziristan and South Waziristan. FATA is the most impoverished region of the nation: it covers only 1.5 per cent of Pakistan's economy, which is chiefly pastoral with some agriculture practised in the region's few fertile valleys. Wheat and maize are the two principal crops but paddy, barley, mustard and even poppies are grown as alternative crops. Fruits are found in abundance and vegetables are also grown. The population comprises chiefly Pashtuns and Afghan refugees.

Gilgit-Baltistan

Gilgit-Baltistan, which was till recently known as the Northern Areas, is situated to the east of Chitral district, in the midst of the world's highest mountains and longest glaciers, and covers an area of 72,971 square km. Sharing borders with China, India and Afghanistan, Gilgit-Baltistan was part of the Kushan Empire in the first to the third centuries AD, and was occupied by Tibet, areas of China and Afghanistan. Presently, the region consists of seven districts—the two Baltistan districts of Skardu and Ghanche, and the five Gilgit districts of Gilgit, Ghizer, Diamer Astore and Hunza-Nagar—a population approaching one million is known for its scattered valley communities. Buddhist and animist, this area converted almost entirely to Islam in the beginning of the twelfth century AD.

   The mountainous terrain makes vegetation almost impossible to grow. The staple food is wheat, while buckwheat and barley are also widely cultivated, and malt grasses consumed. Mostly fruit farmers, all their tribes have distinct identities and lifestyles. Among the ethnic groups living here are Baltis, Hunzakutz, Mughals, Kashmiris, Pashtuns, Tajiks and Mongols.

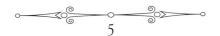

Azad Kashmir

Azad Kashmir is the southern-most political entity within the Pakistani-controlled part of the former princely state of Jammu and Kashmir. It borders the present day Indian-administered state of Jammu and Kashmir to the east (separated from it by the Line of Control); Khyber Pakhtunkhwa to the west; Gilgit-Baltistan to the north; and the Punjab province of Pakistan to the south. With its capital at Muzaffarabad, Azad Kashmir covers an area of 13,297 km^2 and has an estimated population of about four million. Among the major ethnic groups to be found in Azad Kashmir are indigenous Kashmiris, Punjab-origin Kashmiris, Mughals, Pashtuns and Afghans.

Punjab

In sharp contrast to the rugged terrain of Khyber Pakhtunkhwa are the rich and fertile plains of the Punjab. The region has derived its name from five rivers that have influenced the lifestyle of the people of the province in much the same way as the mountains have shaped the culture of the people of Khyber Pakhtunkhwa. These are the tributaries of the Indus River through which the Punjab ('Punj' means 'five' and 'aab' means 'water' in Persian) is irrigated.

Rising in Tibet, the Indus flows down through the Karakoram Mountains that form a part of the northern borders of Pakistan, and continues its journey southwards and

westwards through the heart of the country, carrying and depositing rich alluvium that accounts for Punjab's highly fertile soil. Though not the largest in area, Punjab is the most developed province, and the nerve-centre of Pakistan, with over 60 per cent of Pakistan's population comprising Punjabis. It is also the most progressive part of Pakistan in terms of administration, trade and learning.

Home to numerous villages, small, ancient towns and large cities, the province boasts the ruins of Harappa, a city belonging to the Indus Valley Civilization that flourished about 5000 years ago, and Multan, a city that was born only a few hundred years after the demise of the ancient civilization. It also has the twin cities of Rawalpindi and Islamabad, the latter the modern federal capital of the country, situated on the Potowar Plateau; as well as Lahore, the cultural, architectural and artistic centre of Pakistan, and the country's second largest city.

Lying in the pathway of many of the invasions to which the subcontinent has been subjected through the centuries, one can see the effect of Persian, Greek, Turkish, Sikh, Afghan and Mughal influence on the culture and cuisine of this region. Punjab's population comprises basically indigenous Punjabis that trace their ancestry to pre-Islamic Jat and Rajput castes (Blood 1995) that arrived from Rajputana and Jaisalmer, later inter-marrying with other ethnic groups which came to the area. Other Punjabis trace their heritage to Arabia, Persia, Balochistan, Afghanistan and Kashmir (Blood 1995).

Thus, in contrast to many other areas of the country where people often remained isolated, Punjabis had very diverse origins. The extent of this diversity facilitated their coalescence into a coherent ethnic community that has historically placed great emphasis both on farming and on fighting (Blood 1995). Interaction with one another has resulted in most Punjabis developing similar eating habits, although there are certain delicacies that are associated more with one or the other of the numerous tribes. That is perhaps why, in spite of the Punjab being famous for its cuisine, and Lahorites in particular being known for loving their manna, there are only specific indigenous dishes that the community is famous for.

Another large group of people living in the Punjab—south Punjab to be precise—is Siraikis but they are more a linguistic group than an ethnic one, and hence their cuisine is not distinct. Ethnically they are the same as the natives of Sindh and the rest of the Punjab and trace their ancestry to Jat and Rajput castes. In certain parts of the Punjab Khojas form a notable minority community as do the Baloch, Pashtuns, Afghan refugees and Sikhs.

Balochistan

On the west of the Indus plains lies Balochistan, the largest province of the country in terms of area—about 343,000 square km. It is also the most sparsely populated of Pakistan's provinces—the cause of under-population being its extremely tough terrain. Compared by geologists to the rugged landscape of the planet Mars, Balochistan's terrain has, for centuries, imposed strict limitations on economic activities. In recent years, with the development of the province's rich mineral resources, the situation has been changing.

Balochistan derives its name from one of its three principal ethnic groups, the Baloch; the other two being the Pashtuns and the Brahuis. Some historians believe that the word 'Baloch' is derived from the name of Belus, king of Babylon, while others are of the opinion that Balochs are of Turkman lineage. The nationalist Balochs, on the other hand, ascribe their origin to the earliest Muslim invaders of Persia (Hoiberg and Ramchandani 2000). The Baloch, like the Pashtuns, are a tribal population whose original territory extends beyond the

national borders. Over 70 per cent Baloch live in Pakistan, with the remainder residing in Iran and Afghanistan.

The Brahuis—said to be of Dravidian stock—by contrast, believe that they are indigenous to Balochistan, although, according to one school of thought they are of Turko-Iranian origin (Quddus 1990 and Hughes-Buller 1991). Both the Baloch and the Brahui make their homes in the vast upland deserts stretching southwards and westwards from Balochistan's provincial capital Quetta, to the Arabian Sea. They are predominantly pastoral nomads, breeding sheep, goats and cattle.

The Pashtu-speaking peoples of Balochistan, which include Afghan refugees, are concentrated exclusively in the relatively fertile hills and valleys to the north and north-east of Quetta. From there they continue northwards in an unbroken chain through the tribal belt of the frontier to Peshawar and beyond.

Yet another distinct ethnic group in Balochistan is that of the Makranis, so called according to one theory, because they live on the Makran coast that stretches from Karachi to the Iranian border. The Makranis are a fishing community and according to a folk-tale about their origin, their ancestors were fishermen from Ethiopia who were blown far off-course by a storm and ended up in Balochistan. However, according to some historians they could be the genetic legacy of the African slaves that were brought to the Indo-Pakistan subcontinent by the Arab and European invaders (Sener 2002). Sener feels that there is also the possibility that Makranis could be the descendents of the earliest humans that arrived in Pakistan along the coastal route out of Africa.

Hazaras are also an ethnic group in Balochistan, a Persian-speaking community about whose origin very little is known. It is believed that they migrated in the 1880s from central Afghanistan into British India and settled to the east of Quetta. According to some researchers Hazaras are Mongolian in origin and are descendents of Changez Khan, a theory supported by the similarities in the language and words that Mongols and Hazaras use even today (Poladi 1989). Another plausible theory is that Hazaras were Buddhists that actually lived in Afghanistan at least since the time of the Kushan Dynasty some 2000 years ago.

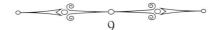

Sindh

Sindh's topography, in vivid contrast to the Punjab's rich, fertile plains comprises vast deserts; forests which are clean of underbrush; and stark, sculptured hills older than the Himalayas. It is also one of the two provinces—the other being Balochistan—that is not landlocked and has a coastline overlooking the Arabian Sea. The coastal fishing waters of Sindh stretch for about 120 miles with sea inlets and many picturesque creeks.

Sindh's geographical position has resulted in it imbibing Iranian, Arab, Central Asian and Indian influences, which, over the years, have been assimilated in the culture of the land. With the Indus Valley Civilization representing the mature phase of the earlier village cultures of Sindh, its chequered history dates back to about five thousand years. In fact, indigenous Sindhis trace their roots as far back as the Indus Valley Civilization (Gidwani 2006). Over the years, the Greeks, Persians, Scythians, Arabs, Mughals and Rajputs left their imprints on the ancient culture of Sindh. Even today, one can see the remnants of the various dynasties that have left their marks on the province, be it in the ancient ruins of Moenjodaro (Mound of the Dead); in the Mughal architecture of its older towns, such as Thatta and Hyderabad; or in the colonial buildings of its largest city, Karachi.

During the British Raj, Sindh, situated in the south of the Punjab, was the neglected hinterland of the Bombay Presidency, with the population dominated by a small number of major landholders (*waderas*). Prior to Partition, about a quarter of the population of Sindh was Hindu, but in the aftermath of the upheaval in the province following Partition most had left for India. Instead, roughly seven million Mohajirs (immigrants) took the places of the fairly well-educated fleeing Hindus and Sikhs in the commercial life of the province, settling primarily in Karachi. Today, the cosmopolitan nature of the province is such that its inhabitants also comprise people of Baloch origin including Makranis, Pashtuns, Punjabis, Sheedis, Zoroastrians, Chinese, Anglo-Indians, Goans, Afghans and Hindus.

Karachi

At the risk of appearing partial I would like to dwell on Pakistan's largest and most cosmopolitan city, Karachi. Its recorded history goes back to the eighteenth century, when it was a small trading post known as Kalachi-jo-Ghote (village of Kalachi). With the development of its harbour it gradually grew into a large city and an important centre of trade and industry. Its selection as capital of Pakistan in 1947 added to its importance and boosted the rate of its growth and development. Although the seat of government was later shifted to Islamabad, Karachi has continued to be the epicentre of commerce and industry. Today, with Karachi boasting a population of about 18 million there is hardly an ethnic community that does not exist in this megapolis. In fact, thanks to the lure of big business and industry this commercial hub has attracted such large numbers of people from all over the country that the original residents of Karachi have become a small minority.

A salad bowl of people from all parts of Pakistan and beyond, Karachi is home to the Makranis and Sheedis, Baloch and Pashtuns, Punjabis and Sindhis, Parsis, Memons, Bohras and Khojas, Urdu-speaking communities from India, Hindus, Bengalis, Afghan refugees, Goans and Anglo-Indian Christians who were once present in sizable numbers, but have now mostly migrated to the west and have been largely replaced by Punjabi Christians. Although the Chinese community too, has in recent years shrunk considerably, it is still mainly concentrated in Karachi and has been responsible for influencing the cuisine of the city, perhaps as much as any of the other communities located here.

2

Cooking the Pakistani Way

While it is generally easy to associate a particular food with a country, so that you may link pasta with Italy, fish and chips with England and shawarma with Lebanon, it is far more difficult to link a specific food item with the whole of Pakistan as it is home to so many diverse ethnic groups. In fact, no food can be regarded as even representative of a whole province, as within each province there are different communities co-existing, each with its own specialties, cooked in a particular way. One can, in fact, go so far as to say that in Pakistan one can learn a lot about one another's culture and ethnic background by the type of food normally cooked in their homes. Having said that, I must admit there are certain features that are common to most types of Pakistani cuisine, giving them a distinct Pakistani flavour. For one, since Islam prohibits pork, most Pakistanis follow this diet restriction rigidly (in fact, pork is not available in the country) and even avoid packaged foods cooked in lard. Also, since alcohol is frowned upon in Islam, its usage in cooking is rare.

All meat (mutton, beef and chicken are the most popular) cooked is halal (permissible for use according to Islamic law) or kosher. Fish is also eaten, particularly in the coastal areas and near rivers and lakes. However, while the majority of Pakistanis have no religious problems eating any kind of fish, some, like the Isnashri Shias and the Bohras do not eat fish without scales, while the former don't eat shell fish, either. Different kinds of fish are popular throughout the country. For instance, in Khyber Pakhtunkhwa, trout and silva are popular river fish. In Sindh where fresh-water fish is available, *palla machli* (elicia) is the rage, in spite of its numerous bones. The coastal city of Karachi is traditionally known for its pomfret, as well as for sear/mackerel, grouper and silver croaker. Now, thanks to greater awareness and continental dishes also becoming popular, fish such as red snapper and sole are also widely consumed.

Wheat being the country's staple crop, the core of all traditional Pakistani meals consists of cereals and grains consumed in the form of bread—*chapatis* or *naans*—without which a

Nans, Chapati and Paratha

meal is generally incomplete. Rice figures as a close contender—if bread is not eaten at a meal, rice takes its place as a staple.

While both rice and bread can be eaten on their own, serving as a cheap stomach-filler and energy provider, they are generally an accompaniment to a main dish, comprising a curry containing meat in one form or the other, *daal* (pulse/split lentil dish) or vegetables. The most common form of meat dishes are meat curry cooked with vegetables—*aloo gosht* (meat with potatoes) being the most popular. Although vegetables are an integral part of the Pakistani diet, few people consume them fresh or lightly cooked. Split lentils or *daal* are traditionally considered inexpensive food source, and typically not served when guests are invited at home.

Also, no matter which community one hails from, one will find that traditional recipes and processes of cooking entail use of fats and oils in meals, which provide the aroma, colour and taste in Pakistani cooking. The oil/fat medium imbibes flavours, aroma and colour from spices and flavour enhancers that are fried in it and passes them on to the main body of the dish. The preparation of curries, vegetable dishes, *daals* and any other item in which gravy is present is considered to be complete only when the cooking fat surfaces to form a layer on top. In fact, without the presence of oil/fat floating on top, the dish is generally not considered to be presentable—although increasing health consciousness is changing that view somewhat in at least the larger cities.

The use of flavour enhancers is also very widespread in Pakistani cooking, regardless of the ethnic group, geographical region and the socio-economic class of the household preparing the food. The five flavour enhancers most commonly used in Pakistani cooking are onions, garlic, ginger, tomatoes and green chillies. One or more of these ingredients are found in almost every Pakistani dish, with onions topping the list.

Aromatics such as ground and whole spices including turmeric, coriander, cumin, red chillies, cinnamon and cardamom, whole grains, oil-rich nuts, and seeds, however, are the ingredients at the heart of Pakistani cooking, making it both immensely flavourful and health-giving. A separate chapter on the spices used in local cuisine has been included

to provide a clearer idea of the ingredients that form an intrinsic part of our gastronomy.

Of the large variety of spices used, many are difficult to clean and handle. Each spice can be prepared and used in many different ways in order to bring out distinctively diverse flavours. A noticeable feature about the local cuisine though, is that village food tends to be simple and uses only the very basic herbs and spices, while food preparation begins to get more elaborate, and usage of ingredients increases in towns and cities.

In Pakistan most housewives prefer to prepare their food from scratch, at the most using single packaged spices—whole or ground—rather than opting for packaged mixed spices. The main reason for this is that the combination of spices used in a dish varies so greatly from family-to-family that most housewives like to adhere to their own recipes, passed down to them by their mothers, mothers-in-law and grandmothers. Thus, dishes even common to most ethnic groups become very household specific in terms of taste and appearance, and vary in identity and flavour from one family to another, preserving traditional family cooking styles. Not surprisingly, using packaged ready-made foods is an alien concept in most local households.

Also, certain traditional utensils will be found in most Pakistani kitchens, without the use of at least one of which it would be difficult to muster the right flavour, especially in certain dishes.

The main utensils used are:

Degchi/pateeli—Cooking pot with no handles, normally used for making curries and rice dishes.

Handi—Thick, round-bottomed, wide-necked cooking pot.

Karahi—Wok-like pan, although slightly heavier, and with a ring-shaped handle on either side. It is usually used for cooking vegetables and for some meat and chicken dishes.

Tawa—A slightly concave, heavy-bottomed griddle pan made of cast iron. Generally used to make *chapatis*, *tawa* is also used to make certain main and side dishes.

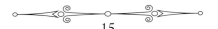

Maghaz (Brain Masala)

Havan dasta (pestle and mortar)—Traditionally made of copper, stone or wood pestles and mortars are also common. Pulverizing spices by using a pestle and mortar helps them to retain more of the flavouring elements than when they are blitzed to a powder in a grinder.

Seel batta — A grooved flat stone and a cylindrical heavy stone piece used to pulverize dry or wet spices, herbs and aromatics such as coriander leaves, garlic and red chillies. The texture of the items crushed with it remains coarser than if they were ground in a blender.

Thaal/thaali/seni — A round steel platter used either to eat food directly from it or to hold different kinds of food placed in small bowls in it.

Sigri — A metal griddle used to place skewers on top and red hot coal below, for barbecuing meats.

Modern gadgets too, have found their way into most urban homes, and even replaced some of the traditional ones, although many prefer to use both, and depending on the item being prepared and time constraints, use one or the other. Some of the common modern gadgets used in urban kitchens particularly are:

Blender — A machine for mixing, liquidizing or pureeing food.

Grinder — A machine used generally for crushing or pulverizing dry ingredients.

Electric beater — A hand-operated machine used for whisking ingredients.

Tenderizing (except by cooking) and marinating are processes rarely used to prepare Pakistani food. Instead, the key to Pakistani cooking lies in the understanding and practice of five fundamental techniques:

1. Bhoonna (frying)

Bhoonna involves the frying of ingredients in an oil or fat medium in an uncovered utensil, on high flame, whilst stirring constantly. An important feature of Pakistani cooking, *bhoonna* is crucial to the preparation of a large number of dishes and is usually done at the

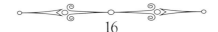

Chargha

beginning of cooking a dish. Where this process is used, onions are added first to the oil/fat, and other flavour enhancers follow once the onions have browned to a desirable degree. During this stage, water is not added at all or added just sparingly to prevent the spices from burning; and stirring is essential so as to prevent the ingredients from sticking to the pot. Considered the key to Mughal cooking (see Mughal cuisine)—which has a strong influence on our cuisine—managing this technique without burning the spices is an art that is perfected with patience and practice. For those learning the ropes, colour and aroma are common cues used to establish that this process is complete. Another sign is that the oil starts to separate from the spices.

There are a number of reasons for adopting this technique in cooking. First and foremost, it kills the raw smell of ingredients. Secondly, it deepens the colour of the spices to richer hues, with the colour also imparted to the fat medium. This process also allows the spices to blend together and all flavours to intermingle and be imbibed by the rest of the ingredients as well. Finally, the constant stirring and frying during this stage helps to break down pieces of tender flavour enhancers, such as onions and tomatoes till they are completely mashed and the gravy is of a smooth consistency.

2. Boiling/Tenderizing

The addition of a large quantity of water to the pot towards the end of the stage of *bhoonna* immediately brings the temperature down, terminating this stage. What follows is the boiling or simmering of ingredients that need to be tenderized—such as meat, vegetables, rice and lentils. Tenderizing cannot be done in oil alone and requires lots of water since the ingredients need to absorb it in order to soften. In cases where the ingredient releases water when cooked, like spinach or chicken, extra water may not be added. Characteristically, this stage of cooking is carried out on a very low heat with the pot covered. As the water content in the pot drops, the oil, which has blended with the water separates and resurfaces.

Moong ki Dal with Baghar

Boiling is also a process commonly used when making *daals*. It involves bringing all ingredients to the boil collectively without first frying the spices and flavour enhancers.

3. Baghar or Tarka (tempering)

This technique is commonly used in the preparation of *daals* and *karhi* (yogurt-based curry) and generally marks the end of a cooking process. It involves frying whole spices and/or flavour enhancers in very hot oil or fat and then pouring the oil along with the contents over the prepared dish. The temperature of the oil is crucial, for if the oil gets too hot, the spices will burn, while if it is not hot enough, the flavour of the spices will not be released. The whole spices used are those that generally pop in oil to release their flavours and aroma (cumin, fenugreek seeds, mustard seeds, whole red chillies, etc.), while flavour enhancers used are those with a very low water content (mostly sliced onion, curry leaves and chopped garlic). The ingredients of *baghar* release their flavour as they hit the oil, and the dish is then covered for a few moments while the ingredients are allowed to brown gently so as to allow the full flavour to be infused. *Baghar* is sometimes performed at the beginning of the cooking process in which case, the rest of the ingredients are added to the oil later, and cooked according to the recipe.

4. Dum (steaming)

Dum involves cooking the dish in its own steam, and is a technique that originated in Persia, where the dish, prepared in a pot called *degchi* (also called *pateeli*) was sealed and buried in the hot sands of the desert to bring forth the best flavours (Sen 2004). Another belief is that the technique became popular in the subcontinent in the eighteenth century, when the famine of 1784 made Nawab Asaf-ud-Daulah of Awadh provide jobs for his subjects by commissioning a monument that was to be built during the day and destroyed at night, thus ensuring a source of continuous employment (Kalra and Gupta 1986/2005). During this process, large quantities of food—rice, meat and spices—were put in a gigantic cooking pot, sealed with dough, and cooked in large double-walled ovens. The gentle steaming that

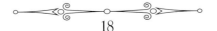

resulted added a deliciously subtle flavour to the food, which would be fed to all the workers. It is said that one day the Nawab sampled a dish cooked in this way and was so impressed that he adapted it for royal banquets and hunts.

Be that as it may, this cooking technique has been in existence at least since the 1500s and has been documented in Abu Fazl's book, *Ain-i-Akbari,* in which various cooking styles in the Royal Kitchen and recipes have been mentioned. According to research it is a cooking technique that was picked up by the formerly nomadic Mughals during their sojourn in areas like modern Uzbekistan, Kazakhstan, Iran and Afghanistan. It was a form of cooking popular in these areas, which allowed semi-prepared food to be cooked in its own steam by placing it in a heavy pot covered with a lid and sealed with a roll of dough wrapped all around its outer edges. The pot would be placed over very low heat—often just smouldering ashes—and live coals would be piled on top of the lid, with the result that the food would get 'baked' slowly with the gentle heat from above and below.

Today, this process is particularly used in the preparation of all rice dishes. Towards the end of cooking, when the rice is almost, but not fully tender, the *degchi* is tightly closed (a weight may be added to the lid to ensure the pot is sealed) and kept on a very low flame. A

Steam cooked Sabziyon ki Biryani
(Vegetable Biryani)

Bihari Kebab (Galavat)

tawa may be placed under the pot to help distribute the heat evenly to its base. If a 'tawa' is not available, the *degchi* can also be placed in a warm oven. At this stage the amount of water in the *degchi* is minimal—just enough to moisten the rice and produce steam in the pot. Steam is produced at the bottom of the pot and as it rises, it fully tenderizes the rice and separates the grains from one another, simultaneously imbibing a delicious, subtle flavour in the food. Perhaps the best example of a dish cooked using this technique is *biryani*. The process of steaming helps the aroma and flavour present in the spiced meat used in the *biryani* to be distributed evenly in the dish.

5. Dhuan/Dhungar (smoking)

This technique imparts a smoky flavour to a dish and is particularly useful when there is no access to a barbecue or *tandoor* (traditional clay oven). A piece of coal is heated until it is red hot and then put on top of a *chapati*, foil piece or a small vessel and placed in the middle of the ingredients to be smoked. Oil is immediately poured over the coal, which releases smoke, at which point the dish is covered tightly and set aside to allow the smoke

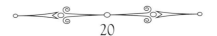

to permeate the food. This technique is normally adopted at the end of the cooking process, giving the food a unique flavour, though sometimes it is done during the cooking process.

6. Galavat

This technique involves the use of softening agents such as *katcha papita* (raw papaya) or *kalmi shora* (saltpetre potassium nitrate) in order to tenderize meat. It is normally employed when marinating beef for certain kebabs.

Another important feature of Pakistani cuisine are the utensils used for cooking. Since every vessel conducts heat in a different way, the flavour of the final product alters depending on the kind of pan used for cooking a particular dish, even if the ingredients in each case are the same. Therefore, many dishes are only prepared in specific kinds of pots and pans in order to acquire their authentic tastes. Some of the commonly used vessels have been described earlier, while others are mentioned in conjunction with the specialties for which they are used.

Bread too, is prepared in a variety of ways, sometimes employing unique methods and cooking aids, some of which one may never have heard about. It is no small wonder then that eating in Pakistan constitutes the single greatest entertainment and pastime of people from all communities and classes.

3

General Meal Patterns

Almost all urban Pakistani households eat breakfast, lunch and dinner daily. While in smaller cities (such as Peshawar, Hyderabad and Multan) lunch is considered the most important meal of the day, in the larger cities, such as Lahore and Karachi, dinner is regarded as the main meal. A major determinant of the main meal is the presence at the mealtime of all family members, particularly male, as well as children. Since distances from work are less in the smaller cities, men leave for work in the morning and generally return home to have lunch with the family, hence, lunches become relatively elaborate affairs. Dinner in smaller cities is a much lighter version of lunch, while in Karachi and Lahore as also in Islamabad, the situation is reversed.

These two sprawling cities, Lahore and Karachi, represent the business centres of the country, and long distances do not allow male family members to return home until office hours are over. It is usually at dinner time that the entire family is together, therefore, dinner is by and large the most important meal of the day in these cities. Late and heavy meals are a traditional practice here and in spite of awareness of its negative consequences few households have attempted to shake off the habit.

However, weekends are the exception when lunch becomes the most important meal of the day in all cities of Pakistan, tending to be somewhat elaborate affairs, with dishes that are cooked on special occasions forming part of the menu.

In villages, on the other hand, the situation is again different. Men in rural areas traditionally work in the fields. Most eat a heavy breakfast at the start of the day, followed by an early dinner when they return home at sunset. Smoke emanating from kitchen fires as tractors roll home at dusk, and the smell of bread cooking in the air are idyllic village scenes typical of the Pakistani countryside. For the villager, breakfast and dinner are simply meal times, and even though the family may be together on both these occasions, the importance of the main meal lies in its function of providing energy rather than being a means for a

family get-together. Lunch is seldom taken at home, and not considered a significant meal by the majority of villagers. It is generally taken as a light meal usually in the fields where a family member brings it to them from home. Meals are normally planned on a daily basis and this trend appears more or less consistently across all ethnic groups, ages and socio-economic categories. The housewife largely carries out decision-making with respect to the menu, although, in some families special-occasion menus are decided in consultation with husband/or children.

The traditional meal structure in the average Pakistani household comprises at least one staple and one main dish (staples are normally eaten with a main dish), with the more affluent households enjoying two staples and at least two main dishes at every meal. The staple normally eaten is grain, in the form of traditional breads, while rice constitutes either as the second or alternate staple. Interestingly, if two staples are served, there is a preference for eating rice first and *roti* later in most communities. Wheat grows more abundantly than rice in Pakistan, is cheaper and more filling, accounting for the traditionally wheat-based diet found in the country. The main dish in affluent households is meat-based—whether mutton, beef, chicken or fish—and if two main dishes are served, then the other is usually a vegetable or *daal*.

Desserts are not normally a part of everyday meals and it is generally over weekends or on special occasions that sweet dishes are served. However, even this tradition of ending a special meal with a dessert has its origins in Arabia. *Paan* (betel leaf) is popular after meals to digest food, as are cardamoms, aniseed, betel nut and coriander.

Chai or tea—usually boiled with lots of milk and sugar—is a very popular drink consumed in all seasons and practically throughout the day, in the cities as well as in some of the villages. While the British may have certainly played a role in boosting its popularity, they were by no means the first to introduce this beverage to the subcontinent, as the northern parts of Pakistan have been exposed to tea from time immemorial thanks to its proximity with China, and invasions from Central Asia. It is common to serve *chai* in Pakistan as a welcome gesture to guests. A variant is *doodh-patti* which is basically tea cooked in milk instead of water.

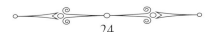

Til Walay Naan (Sesame Seed Naan)

Staples

Breads

A large variety of breads (*roti*) are consumed throughout Pakistan, some more exotic and richer than others, although those are normally reserved for special occasions. Daily bread is usually cooked at home on a *tawa* (a slightly concave heavy-bottomed griddle pan made of cast iron) from unleavened basic dough made from whole-wheat flour (*gehon ka aata*), water and salt. The result is a light, thin, flat round bread called *chapati* or *phulka*.

History has it that the Indus Valley Civilization, which emerged some 5000 years ago on the banks of the River Indus, introduced this form of bread. The existence of granaries at Moenjodaro, Harappa and Lothal (all ancient cities) further testify that wheat was the basic commodity playing a pivotal role in the barter system prevalent in those days. At a time when people in Europe lived in caves (Gidwani 2006) the Indus Valley people had a centralized granary where they they would deposit wheat and barley and which might have acted as the economic equivalent of our modern day State Bank (Pruthi 2004).

While many Pakistani homes consume this form of whole wheat bread thrice a day, *parathay* (fried unleavened bread) are more popular for breakfast both in urban and rural centres, as are *puris* which are deep fried, but lighter than the *parathay*. There is a preference for the baked bread loaf/toast at breakfast in such cities as Islamabad, Karachi and Lahore. Although other urban and semi-urban centres as well as some rural areas also use the bakery bread, it is in these cities, which have had greater exposure to western tastes in general, that one finds a strong foreign influence on the Pakistani palate. Larger cities normally mean a fast-paced lifestyle and the use of bread loaf is more convenient and less time consuming than making *chapatis*. For the same reason, rusks are popular at breakfast in the larger cities.

Tandoori naan, rarely made at home other than in Peshawar, is normally bought as an alternate to homemade *chapati*. Its popularity can be traced to as far back as the ubiquitous *chapatis*, for remnants of a *tandoor* (clay oven) have been discovered from excavation at the

Indus Valley sites. However, the Persian-speaking central Asian nations—particularly the regions around Afghanistan, Uzbekistan, Iran and Tajikistan—have also for centuries been consuming *naan* the way we know it, and it is believed that through conquests and trade, the basic recipe of the *naan* found its way to the subcontinent. Interestingly, *tandoors* started out in the Punjab as social institutions as much as a means of cooking. Since not all homes could accommodate *tandoors*, communal *tandoors* were used by people to cook bread from flour kneaded at home, offering them the opportunity to meet neighbours and catch up with news and gossip at the same time.

Naan is eaten for breakfast only in Peshawar, but is widely consumed at other meal times all over the country. Thicker and spongier than the *chapati* and usually made out of white flour, the *naan* is made of dough containing yeast. The dough is kneaded for a few minutes; then set aside to rise for a few hours. Once risen, the dough is divided into balls, patted into shape—flat, round or tear-shaped—and pushed through a hole into a large, spherical clay/earth oven, called a *tandoor*. About four feet deep, a bed of charcoal heats it. The dough, plastered to the oven wall, is removed with a pair of long metal spikes when ready.

The most common derivatives of *naan* are the Peshawari and Kashmiri *naan*. These are filled with a mixture of nuts and raisins and are much broader and thicker than the normal *naans*. By adding variations to the original recipe in the form of flavourings or fillings, both the *paratha* and the *naan* can take on exotic dimensions. And so it is that there are varieties of stuffed *naans* such as those with mince meat, chicken, or potato; and flavoured *naan* such as those with garlic or butter. Popular sprinklings on *naan* include cumin, sesame and nigella seeds.

Other bread varieties include *sheermal* (prepared with milk and butter); *taftan* (a soft, leavened flour bread with saffron and cardamom powder); *Kandahari naan* (long bread); *kulcha* (bread sprinkled with sesame seeds); *bhature* (soft and fluffy, fried bread); *roghni naan* (sprinkled with sesame seeds and covered with minute amounts of oil); and *Bumbaiya naan* (thick, soft and spongy bread). *Baqerkhani* is another favourite (a red, layered roti made with white flour and *mawa*—which is whole dried milk).

Yakhni Pulao

Varieties of *parathay* include those stuffed with potatoes, mince meat, radish, turnips, onions or corn. Generally, these variations are reserved for special occasions. Occasionally, *roti* is also made with gram flour (*besan*), millet (*bajra*), maize (*makai*), sorghum (*jowar*) or barley (*joh*) and served with special entrees.

Rice

Rice, rarely eaten at breakfast, is usually consumed in its plain boiled form in accompaniment with a main dish with gravy. Culturally, rice is eaten just tender and not overcooked, with each individual rice grain separate from the other. Overcooked rice, which clumps and becomes sticky, is generally viewed as sub-standard and unpalatable. Basmati rice, favoured for its long fine grains and aroma, is considered the choicest of all varieties of rice. It grows only in the subcontinent and has a high price tag, but is preferred—especially when the housewife plans her menu for important dinners and special occasions. Needless to say, the quality of basmati rice also varies—the finer and more aromatic is naturally more expensive.

On special occasions, rice can be cooked in many exotic styles, varying from the relatively simple *pulao*—rice cooked with fried flavour enhancers, spices and vegetables—to a rich meat *pulao* or *biryani* which combines rice with meat and could constitute a main meal eaten on its own.

Main dish

While staples can constitute a meal by themselves, the main course is never eaten on its own. For breakfast, a large number of households prefer to eat eggs as the main dish, which are normally either fried or prepared as omelettes—frequently with green chillies, onions, coriander leaves and tomatoes—while many eat leftovers of the night before. In semi-urban areas such as Hyderabad, Peshawar and Multan, a variety of vegetarian dishes, such as *aloo baingan* (potato and eggplant), *aloo bhujia* (potato curry) and *chanay/cholay* (chickpeas curry) are also popular for breakfast. As a norm meat dishes are not consumed at breakfast, but when they are, the ones preferred, especially on special occasions include *shami kebab* (minced beef patty), *qeema* (minced meat), *kaleji* (liver), *maghaz* (brain), *paya* (goat trotters), and *nihari* (beef stew cooked with bones).

For lunch and dinner, a choice of a wide variety of curries, *daal* and vegetable dishes comprise the traditional cuisine, and many affluent households serve at least two dishes at a meal—generally one meat dish, either wet or dry, which becomes the main dish, and one vegetable or *daal* platter, which is treated as a side dish. However, while the majority of Pakistani dishes contain meat in one form or another (whether beef, mutton, chicken or fish) there are a large number of homes that cannot afford or do not serve meat, especially in the rural areas. In such cases the *daal* and vegetable dish alone serves as the main course, eaten with the desired staple. Normally, the drier the item, the greater the likelihood of eating it with bread, while the curries are eaten with rice.

The ubiquitous *daal* has probably been around since mid-third millennium BC, since lentils were cultivated on the fertile basin surrounding the Indus (Southworth 2005). Simple to cook, all it requires is the split lentils to be boiled and simmered before giving it a *tarka* of one's choice—generally with either a combination of whole red chillies, sliced onions, curry leaves, garlic and spices, or any of these. The *daals* most commonly used are golden yellow lentils or split peas (*chana*), split moong beans (*moong*), split pink lentils (*masoor*), white lentils (*maash* or *urad*) and deep yellow lentils (*arhar*). There are tons of *daal* recipes around, using different spices, lemon juice, tamarind, raw mango, or mangostein (*kokum*) to add to their flavour. Meat or vegetables are also added, if they can be afforded, to make mouth-watering dishes that can be eaten with either *roti* or rice.

Vegetables such as potato, pumpkin, eggplant, bitter gourd, okra, and spinach which are available throughout the year, or seasonal veggies such as cauliflower, peas and carrots are also abundantly eaten practically throughout the country. Single vegetables are more popular than mixed vegetables and include the popular okra and potato. Mixed vegetables often contain potatoes combined with other vegetables such as pumpkin, cauliflower and peas. The most common form of meat dish is meat cooked with a vegetable, in particular *aloo gosht* (meat with potatoes). Popular variations include *palak gosht* (meat with spinach), *kadoo gosht* (meat with pumpkin) and *aloo qeema* (minced meat with potatoes),

Chutneys and Raita

while combinations with eggplant, bitter gourd, okra, rutabaga or mustard greens are not uncommon.

Accompaniments

These are a selection of relishes and side dishes that do not constitute a meal on their own. They serve to complement the flavours of the main meal, titillate the palate and lessen the heat of the spices. They include salads, soups, butter, yogurt, *raita*, *kachoomar*, pickles (*achars*), chutneys, ketchup, and packaged sauces. Mangoes (in season) are also consumed as accompaniments to the main meal in many households that can afford to serve fruits. Beverages, such as milk, tea, juice, green tea and *lassi* (buttermilk) are also regarded as accompaniments. These may or may not be a part of the regular meal but the likelihood of their presence becomes higher over the weekends and on special occasions.

Achars (Pickles)

Once exclusively made at home, pickles are now generally bought ready-made by households, especially in the cities, where few people have the patience or the inclination to go through the tedious procedure of making them at home. Variations include *keri ka achar* (made from raw mangoes), lemon *achar*, turnip, carrot, and cabbage pickles.

Chutneys

The word 'chutney' comes from the Urdu word *chaat na*, meaning 'to lick'. So, essentially chutney is an accompaniment that is regarded to be finger-licking good. They can be made either by grinding fresh ingredients or by cooking them. Chutneys are always vegetarian and have a sour, tangy taste, even when they include sweet ingredients like fruits—such as mangoes and apricots. Variations include mango chutney, apricot chutney, herb chutney, coconut chutney, green chutney (made with grated coconut, green chillies, lemon juice, mint and coriander leaves), tomato and green chillies chutney, and sweet date and tamarind chutney.

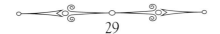

Raita

Raitas

Usually eaten with *pulaos*, *raita* is made with whipped yogurt and mint with seasoning.

Kachumers

A raw vegetable accompaniment, inspired by the Turkish yogurt with cucumber side dish, the Pakistani version usually includes both onion and cucumber and can be served with or without yogurt. Instead of yogurt, vinegar is often used.

Desserts

Mithais or sweetmeats, the *desi* option to pastries, are popular at any time of the day, more so after meals or as part of tea-time snacks. Although during weekdays desserts are usually not included in the menu, they often form part of the weekend and special occasion meals, adding a festive touch to the menu. In fact, with *mithai* an important part of the Pakistani lifestyle there is rarely a happy or sad occasion when it is not served—it is not surprising that sweetmeat shops catering mind-boggling varieties have sprung up practically throughout the country.

Mithais by and large tend to be traditional milk-based puddings such as *sheerkhurma* (made with vermicelli and dried dates, which gives it its name—*khurma* means dates), *kheer* (made with rice), *halwas* (a variety of sweets made with different ingredients), or even western-style custard. Seasonal fruit or vegetable-based desserts are also common. Most households continue to cook Pakistani desserts in *ghee* (clarified butter), despite the common knowledge that it has a higher cholesterol content as they feel that only *ghee* can provide the right flavour to these special traditional dishes.

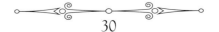

The history of these delectable delights dates back to the Vedic era, when the first recipes emerged incorporating ingredients such as fruits, vegetables, grains, dairy products and honey. Later, as more and more people from different parts of the world travelled to the region, they introduced many new ingredients which became a part of the local *halwas* and *mithais*. However, it wasn't until the Mughal era that *mithais* such as *ladoos* (a sweet that is often prepared to celebrate festivals or household events such as weddings) evolved and became popular practically throughout the country. *Ladoos* are made of flour and other varied ingredients formed into balls, which are dipped in sugar syrup. Other popular *mithais* include *gulab jamans* (deep fried, milk-based balls dipped in sugar syrup), *qalakand* (made with cheese and milk) and *jalebis* (syrupy, deep fried pretzel-shaped sweet).

Gulab Jamans

Jalebis

4

Commonly Used Ingredients in Local Cuisine

Spices

Nothing characterizes Pakistani cooking more than its vivid and imaginative use of dried spices, possibly because so many of the plants from which the spices are derived are either native to the subcontinent or thrive in this environment. Of course, 'spicy' doesn't necessarily mean chilli, although, the latter is often an important ingredient in Pakistani cooking. Just as salt and pepper levels can be adjusted to suit tastes, the quantity of spices may be altered without compromising the authenticity of the dish in any way.

There are many ways of employing spices. You can use them whole, ground, roasted, or fried. A single spice can completely alter the flavour of a dish and combinations of several in varying proportions can produce totally different colours and textures.

The following are some of the commonly used spices in Pakistani cuisine:

Cardamom (*Elettaria cardamomum*) *Elaichi*

The second most expensive spice after saffron, cardamom pods can be used with or without their husks and have a slightly pungent but aromatic taste. Featuring prominently in dishes of Mughal origin, they add fragrance to the dishes. They come in two types—green and black. The green pods, which are the more expensive variety, are small in size, and can be used for both sweet and savoury dishes. The black, which are not true cardamom but from plants of the related *Amomum* and *Afromomum genus*, are cheaper, larger, coarser and less aromatic, and only used for savoury dishes. Cardamom pods can be chewed as breath fresheners and digestive aids, and it is believed that they sharpen the mind and combat

nausea, headaches, fevers, coughs, asthma, piles and eye diseases. The seeds are supposed to be of particular assistance against urine retention.

Chilli (*Capsicum frutescens*) *Saabit sookhi lal mirch*

Dried red chillies constitute an important ingredient in Pakistani cuisine. They can be used either whole or crushed or as chilli powder. Whole dried chillies are usually fried in oil before use and are popular in *tarkas* of dishes such as *karhi* and *daal*. They are extremely fiery and break easily once cooked, spewing their seeds into the broth. The crushed and powdered chillies, however, tend not to have the potency and flavour of the whole pods. Red chillies are healthy as they are low in sodium and very low in saturated fat and cholesterol. They are also said to be good for digestive ailments.

Mixed spices *Garam masala*

This is a combination of certain spices and can be used either ground or whole in Pakistani cooking. Normally, cumin, cloves, cinnamon sticks, cardamom pods and black pepper are combined when making ground *garam masala*. Many people prefer to grind their own *garam masala* at home. Bay leaves are often interspersed when using whole *garam masala*. It is very potent in its powdered form and is used very sparingly and only at the end of preparing a dish, usually as a garnish. However, whole *garam masala* is generally used at the beginning of the preparation of a dish and lends a wonderful warmth and richness to food. *Garam masala* is generally used with meat and rice but rarely with fish or vegetables, as the combination of powerful spices is considered too strong for delicate flavours.

Cinnamon (*Cinnamomum verum*) *Darchini*

Cinnamon is used both in its stick form (strips of bark rolled together), and ground to a powder, and is popular for its flavour and the aroma it imparts to the dishes. As a culinary ingredient, ground cinnamon is used as part of *garam masala* and is used to season meat, poultry, fish and rice dishes. On its own, cinnamon sticks are used to add fragrance to such simple village fare as a dish of boiled rice and lentils, and to the elaborate dishes of

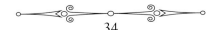

aristocratic cuisine. Since cinnamon is delicate in taste, it is also used to flavour desserts. Cinnamon is considered to be a natural system cleanser and an aid to digestion. It is also antibacterial and helps relieve congestion.

Cloves (*Eugenia caryophylus*) *Laung*

Cloves lend their warming pungency to many sweet and savoury dishes and are usually added whole in Pakistani cooking. Ground cloves form part of most *garam masala* mixtures. The essential oil from cloves has long been used as a natural pain-killer, particularly against toothache. It also aids digestion and relieves flatulence and is used as an antiseptic. It is also known for lowering cholesterol levels in the blood.

Coriander seeds (*Coriandrum sativum*) *Dhania*

The aromatic, brown seeds of the coriander plant have a sharp flavour and are roasted and crushed to form the spices for almost all savoury dishes. They are used whole, coarsely ground or in powder form. Ground coriander seeds are often mixed with ground cumin to form *dhania-zeera* powder (coriander-cumin powder). They are known for their beneficial effect on the digestive system and for treating insomnia.

Cumin (*Cuminum cyminum*) *Zeera*

Zeera (Cumin)

There are two main varieties of cumin fruits or 'seeds' as they are often referred to—light brown (*sufaid zeera*) and black (*kala zeera*). The flavour of cumin, like that of most seeds, is greatly improved by roasting or frying before use, and so generally the fruits of the light brown cumin are roasted and powdered to form the spices for almost all savoury dishes, and are often mixed with ground coriander seeds to form *dhania-zeera* powder, used in most curries. However, they are also used whole and coarsely ground in many dishes and widely used for flavouring lentils, vegetable curries, pickles and breads.

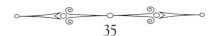

The smaller and thinner black cumin fruits (often erroneously referred to as caraway or occasionally, nigella) have a stronger and sweeter aromatic flavour than the brown ones, and are mostly used to flavour rice. The cumin fruit is known for its digestive properties, especially when roasted, and is also an effective antidote to morning sickness.

Turmeric *(Curcuma longa) Haldi*

Turmeric is always used in ground form (a fine yellow powder) obtained by boiling and drying the stem of the *curcuma longa* plant. It is an essential ingredient in curry powder and is used in several local dishes, enhancing their flavour and giving them a golden colour. It is mildly aromatic (with scents of orange or ginger) and is known to help mask fish odours. Turmeric also has numerous medicinal qualities. It is used to control blood pressure and cholesterol, treat indigestion, stomach and liver ailments (by adding it to milk) as well as to heal sores. It is also believed to be effective in combating Alzheimer's disease and is used extensively to improve complexion and as a depilatory. It is also said to cure itching, skin diseases and conjunctivitis.

Fenugreek seeds *(Trigonella foenum-graecum) Methi dana*

The flavour of the whole, dried, flat yellow seeds is almost unpalatably sharp, but improves when the seeds are lightly fried. The seeds are used in many ready-made curry powders, and add relish and zest to all foods. They are particularly delicious with potatoes. Rich in vitamin A, fenugreek is considered to have the ability to cleanse the body of toxins. It is said to be effective in lowering blood pressure and improving the digestive, respiratory and nervous systems.

Mustard seeds *(Brassica nigra) Rai dana*

These seeds, either black or yellow, are round and have a sharp flavour. They are used for flavouring curries, particularly fish and vegetable, and pickles, and develop a delicious nutty taste when fried in oil. Mustard seeds stimulate the appetite and are said to be good for the skin.

Nutmeg (*Mystica Fragrans*) *Jaifal*

Nutmeg has a rich, sweet, warm and aromatic flavour which is at its best when freshly ground. It is traditionally thought to have general tonic properties, especially for the digestive system, heart, brain and reproductive organs. It is normally used in desserts, especially 'kheer'. Used in small dosages nutmeg can reduce flatulence, aid digestion, improve the appetite and treat diarrhoea, vomiting and nausea.

Mace *Javithry*

Mace is a spice made from the waxy red covering which covers nutmeg seeds. The flavour is similar to that of nutmeg, with a hint of pepper and a more subtle taste which can become overwhelming at the hands of heavy-handed cooks. Mace is available in both whole and ground form, and it has a wide range of uses: from flavouring desserts such as *kheer* to savoury items such as roast meats. It is used to treat gastrointestinal complaints, toothache, nausea and depression, and has analgesic and aphrodisiacal properties.

Onion seeds (*Allium cepa*) *Kalonji*

Black in colour and triangular in shape, these tangy seeds are used both in pickles and vegetable curries. They are supposed to enhance the secretion of milk in expectant mothers. Scientific studies have shown that they contain potent sexual hormones, stimulants, urine and bile diuretics, digestive enzymes, antacids and sedatives, among other useful compounds.

Peppercorns (*Piper nigrum*) *Kali mirch*

One of the oldest spices known to humankind, pepper is probably the most common flavouring after salt, in both western and eastern cooking. Pepper stimulates the appetite and digestion, encourages perspiration and has considerable antioxidant and antibacterial properties. It is used for the alleviation of cold, cough and bronchial complaints. Its main culinary function is as a preservative. It is a frequent ingredient in Pakistani cuisine, usually in the form of whole peppercorns in rice, meat and pickles. Powdered, it is one of the main ingredients of the mixed spices that are the basis of curry powders.

Pomegranate seeds *(Punica granatum) Anar dana*

Valued for their sweet and sour flavour, ground pomegranate seeds are used as a souring agent in Pakistani cooking, particularly in chutneys, and vegetable and pulse dishes. Pomegranates are high in vitamin C and fibre, and contain the minerals iron, potassium and calcium. Other nutrients include vitamin A, vitamin E and folic acid.

Poppy seeds *(Papaver somniferum) Khus khus*

Tiny dried seeds of the opium poppy, poppy seeds are an ancient spice and have no narcotic properties, because the fluid contained in the bud that becomes opium is present only before the seeds are fully formed. The delicious nutty flavour of poppy seeds is always better when the seeds have first been roasted. They are used, often whole, to flavour curries and coat savoury items. Ground to a paste with water, poppy seeds are sometimes used as a thickening agent. They are recommended in many prescriptions for tonics as their mineral contents include calcium and phosphorus.

Carom seeds *Ajwain*

Carom seeds are pale beige coloured and look like a smaller version of cumin fruits. They are highly fragrant and smell and taste like thyme, but with a stronger flavour. They are normally used in their seed form and are rarely used as a powder. Carom seeds are used mostly to flavour vegetable dishes, and in pickles because of their preservative qualities. They are believed to aid digestion; relieve symptoms of cold; and ease rheumatic pain.

Saffron *(Crocus sativus) Zafran*

The world's most expensive spice is saffron. Luckily, only a small quantity is needed to flavour and impart colour and fragrance to a dish, whether sweet or savoury. To bring out

the flavour, saffron is usually lightly roasted and soaked in milk. It is used extensively in Mughal dishes such as *qorma* and *biryani* and in desserts such as *shahi tukray*. Widely regarded as an aphrodisiac, especially when dissolved in milk, saffron is also said to relieve respiratory congestion. It is used in pastes to improve complexion and is reputed to purify the mind.

Chaat masala

This is a concoction of different spices used in a variety of *chaats* (subcontinental savoury snack) to enhance their flavour. Dried coriander and cumin are roasted and ground into a fine powder and mixed with equal quantities of ground dry red chillies, dry mango powder and black rock salt (*kala namak*). A double helping of black pepper is also added to the mix. *Chaat masala* is extremely health-giving as nearly all its components aid in digestion.

Tamarind (*Tamrindus indica*) Imli

Tamarind is integral to Pakistani cuisine and is used in many curries, sauces, pickles, as well as in *imli ki chutney* which is an essential ingredient in *chaat*. The pulp is rich in calcium, vitamin C, phosphorus and iron and is considered a useful cooling agent during fever. Tamarind is a remedy for ulcers because of its antiseptic properties and can also be rubbed on to alleviate sunburns.

Aromatics

These are vegetables that are mostly used, like herbs and spices, for their flavouring properties, rather than consumed as food. These include:

Green Chillies (*Capsium frutescens*) Hari mirch

Fresh green chillies and their riper red counterparts are used in Pakistani cooking both as an ingredient and as a garnish. Other than imparting their own richly aromatic flavour and

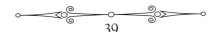

Ginger and Garlic

spice, they also have the power to bring out the flavour of ingredients around them. Fresh chillies are packed with vitamins A, B and C and are also potent stimulants to the system, which are highly antibacterial and help normalize blood pressure.

Garlic (*Allium sativum*) *Lassan*

Ground garlic is frequently used in curries, especially in conjunction with ginger, while whole cloves are sometimes added to lentil dishes. Garlic is as known for its medicinal properties as for its flavour. It is antiseptic and powerfully antibacterial when raw, and even when cooked it helps the body eliminate toxins and lowers cholesterol. It is also used to treat rheumatism and high blood pressure.

Ginger (*Zingiber officinale*) *Adrak*

An important ingredient used in many curries, preserves and chutneys, it is usually peeled and then cut into matchstick shreds, or used as a pulp. It acts as a tenderizer when applied sparingly to meat and also contributes a freshness and distinctive heat to meat dishes. A potent stimulant, ginger aids the digestive processes. It alleviates travel sickness and vertigo and is also recommended for treatment of colds and sore throats.

Herbs

Curry Leaves (*Murraya koenigii*) *Kari patta*

These are principally used to flavour lentil dishes and vegetable curries.

Fenugreek (*Trigonella foenum-graecum*) *Methi*

Methi leaves are used to flavour both meat and vegetarian dishes.

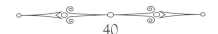

Mint (Mentha) *Podina*

The fresh taste of mint leaves has ensured its popularity in Pakistani cuisine, particularly in chutneys and *raitas*. It works very well in tandem with fresh coriander and is especially used in dishes incorporating lamb and yogurt.

Bay Leaves (*Laurus nobilis/Cassia Lignea*) *Tej patta*

One of the most ancient of herbs used in cooking, the leaves of the bay or laurel tree are often used to flavour exotic rice dishes like *biryani*. In the coastal areas it is also used as a seasoning on fish gravies, lentils and vegetable greens. It is supposed to be of assistance in cardiac disorders.

Fresh Coriander (*Coriandrum sativum*) *Hara dhania*

One of the most popular culinary plants of Pakistan, its leaves are chopped and sprinkled over curried meats and vegetables as garnish. Used also as an ingredient, its zesty flavour blends well with chillies and that's why it's adopted in dishes which are chilli hot. The plant is particularly effective as a diuretic and has a reputation of breaking fever.

Garnishes

In Pakistani cooking, the most common form of garnishing is chopped coriander, followed by sliced onions, green chillies and tomatoes.

When garnishing desserts, ground cardamoms, almonds and pistachios or slivered almonds and pistachios, and currants are preferred. *Varq* (sterling silver leaf) used to be a highly popular garnish and was imbibed enthusiastically in the days of the Nawabs, as it enjoyed the reputation of having aphrodisiac properties. However, over the years, inflation and health concerns have made its usage considerably less. Nonetheless, it is still used to decorate *mithai* on special occasions and is a sign of opulence. Making *varq* is a very laborious process in which small, thin, coin-like pieces of silver are placed between layers of leather and paper and beaten for hours to flatten and transform it to wafer-like foil.

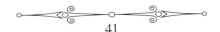

5

Culinary Evolution

While some things have undoubtedly not changed even since the days of the Indus Valley Civilization, over the years the culinary scene in Pakistan has undergone a radical transformation in many ways. Let's first take a look at the similarities in the cuisine of the past with present-day gastronomy. Aside from the fact that wheat *chapatis* were also eaten by the people of the Indus Valley there is evidence in history that sesame and eggplant were grown and humped cattle was domesticated. Turmeric, cardamom, black pepper and mustard were also harvested in the region.

Many recipes first emerged during the initial Vedic period, when the subcontinent was still heavily forested and agriculture was complemented with game hunting and forest produce. Over time, some segments of the population embraced vegetarianism, a practice that gained popularity as the climate was conducive to growing a variety of fruits, vegetables, and grains which could easily be grown throughout the year. Hence, in Vedic times, a normal diet consisted of fruit, vegetables, meat, grain, dairy products and honey.

Later, a series of invasions by Persians, Greeks, Central Asians, Arabs, Turks, Afghans, Sikhs and the Mongols, ultimately giving way to the establishment of the Mughal Empire, and later British colonization, diversified subcontinental tastes and meals. While Islamic rule introduced rich gravies, *pulaos*, and non-vegetarian fare such as kebabs; Mughlai cuisine, strongly influenced by Persian and Turkic cuisines of Central Asia, introduced creamy and buttery curries. The Mughals were by and large, great patrons of cooking. Their courts also attracted scholars and adventurers from the entire Islamic world, and in the process many new ingredients and dishes from the Middle East and North Africa were introduced into the court cuisine. Lizzie Collingham says about the cooks at Akbar's court: 'Each brought with him his own regional techniques and recipes. The cooks learned from each other and out of this vibrant synthesis of culinary styles emerged a core repertoire of dishes that constituted a new Mughlai cuisine.'

Lavish dishes were prepared during their reigns, which were developed and perfected later by the Nizams (sovereigns) of Hyderabad state who added their own style of cooking to the dishes.

Influence of traders such as the Arabs and Portuguese also became apparent on the cuisine. While previously leafy greens known as *saag*—which may include the leaves of mustard, fenugreek, radish, chickpea plants and spinach—eggplant, bitter gourd, bottle gourd and taro were the main indigenous vegetables that locals were familiar with, local cuisine began to absorb New World vegetables which had been unheard of till then, such as tomato, chilli, okra, and potato, introduced by the Portuguese, as important foods. The British, meanwhile, introduced temperate European vegetables such as cabbage, cauliflower, lettuce and green beans. The Portuguese and British also introduced to the locals, among other things, cooking techniques like baking, so that many a baked item like pastries, cakes and patties became a part of the local cuisine.

After Pakistan came into being and the many different communities that made it their home all contributed their traditional dishes to the local fare, Pakistani cuisine became richer and more varied. But while the variety in cuisine has increased phenomenally, traditional cooking methods have remained largely the same over the years, especially in villages and smaller towns. Pakistan's cities and larger towns, however, have undergone some subtle, and many blatant changes. Perhaps, the most significant is the use of electronic gadgets when preparing *masalas*. While traditional methods of grinding spices are used in villages where no alternative is available, only those families in cities depend on time-tested methods of pulverizing masalas that feel authentic flavours are lost when using modern gadgets. Otherwise, practically all affluent households in the cities and towns now employ the use of electric grinders, blenders and the like.

Also, while rural areas still largely employ traditional earthen stoves for cooking, urban areas have progressed from using simple single-burner gas stoves to steel ovens of either local or imported variety. The use of refrigerators and microwave ovens has also been on the increase in the cities, although, the latter are employed more for heating purposes than for cooking.

Initially, poor means of communication and transportation had restricted the usage of ingredients in remote areas especially, so that the inhabitants of the mountainous northern areas or Thar Desert, for instance, had access only to those limited, hardy food items that could be grown in such difficult terrains. Often, food that could last for several days and be eaten without heating was preferred. Today, the scenario has changed to a large extent and practically the entire country has access to a variety of fresh fruits and vegetables grown in and transported from other areas.

Another phenomenon that has brought a radical change in the eating habits and availability of food items, particularly in the cities, is the advent of the deep freezer. Not only has it made it possible for seasonal fruits like apples to be available the year round, but it has also been responsible for the introduction of packaged frozen foods, such as rolls, *samosay*, drumsticks and much more, not to mention frozen meats. Whereas once meat was only purchased fresh, and chicken often bought live and cut at home, now choice pieces of packaged frozen meat—chicken breasts, drumsticks, etc.—are popular so that a whole chicken need not be bought at all if only a specific part is required by recipe.

Ghee, particularly *desi ghee* which was once considered the only acceptable fat medium in which to cook local cuisine has rapidly fallen in grace thanks to its high cholesterol content, and has been largely replaced by oils, the most popular being Canola and Sunflower. However, even detractors of *ghee* admit there is a definite sacrifice in taste when using oil, and still prefer to use the former when preparing special dishes like *biryani* or *halwa*.

Desi (farm) chickens and eggs which were once the only kind available have now been almost entirely replaced by the ubiquitous broiler chickens and eggs because of their relative affordability.

Huqqa—a single or multi-stemmed instrument for smoking tobacco in which the smoke is cooled and filtered by passing through water—was once popular as much with the nobility as with villagers, and was an integral part of many a middleclass household. Today, its usage is almost entirely restricted to villages, and has been replaced in the cities by its close cousin introduced in the Middle East, the *sheesha*, which incorporates fruit flavours.

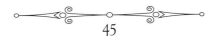

Greater general awareness about foreign cuisines among the masses has also resulted in the demand for, and subsequently the supply of a large number of vegetables and spices that were previously unavailable. Although still not used in local cuisine, the availability of these ingredients have made the preparation of authentic western dishes much easier, and thanks to a growing number of cooking shows on satellite television, more and more people are becoming familiar with the methods of preparing such dishes. Among the many vegetables now available in the cities are broccoli, parsley, chives, avocado, kaffir leaves, basil leaves, capers, jalapeno, iceberg lettuce and celery. What's more, packaged spices such as thyme, oregano, and dried rosemary are now being produced locally as well.

Some changes have also taken place in the production of fruits, making it possible for a greater variety of fresh juices and desserts to be made now. One important factor that triggered the growth of some of these fruits in Pakistan was the division of the country in 1971. Prior to the fall of East Pakistan fruits like leeches, coconuts and pineapples were grown basically in the eastern wing of the country, and hence, though available, were expensive to come by in West Pakistan. After 1971, for a good many years these fruits became an imported luxury in Pakistan until effort was made to grow them locally, with the result that now they are grown in abundance. In fact, the same holds true for *paan*, which was also once produced only in the eastern part of the country, and was a rarity in West Pakistan. Great variety of mangoes began to be developed, some brought from India. Among the other fruits that have recently begun to be grown locally are strawberries and cherries.

While modernization has affected the food variety in the country, it has also brought changes in the eating styles of the general populace so that, whereas, in the days of yore people only ate on *dastarkhwans*—linen spread on the floor on which diners sat and ate food—today dining tables have to a large extent replaced the erstwhile meals on *dastarkhwans*. Similarly, while most people continue to use their fingers to eat food—generally eaten with the right hand, and in case of curries, *rotis* are used to scoop it up—and the usage of forks and knives is still limited to the upper-income groups in cities, spoons are now more widely used by the general populace for eating semi-solid food items like *haleem*, and even for rice, than ever before.

The result of the increase in sophistication in the culinary taste of city dwellers has resulted in a change in the restaurant scene in the country as well. For instance, in Karachi, whereas once Malabari restaurants—serving south-western Indian cuisine from Malabar, thus its name—and Iranian cafes were the rage among people from diverse income groups, today they have been replaced by open-air *dhabas* that serve a wide variety of cuisine that may range from barbecue food to *karahis*; and from burgers to Chinese fare. The vegetarian restaurants that used to cater to the large number of Hindus settled in the country, and the coffee houses that were frequented by the intelligentsia have disappeared entirely and *niche* or theme restaurants have sprung up to tantalize the taste buds of those who can afford to frequent them. Whereas lunch and dinner were the only meals generally served at eateries, so that restaurants would be closed other than at specific meal times, today they are normally open from morning till night and also serve breakfast, brunch on weekends, and tea/snacks through out the day.

International fast-food franchises have also sprung up in many parts of the country, so much so that even railway stations have their outlets. Take-away and delivery services, a relatively recent phenomena, has also impacted the eating habits of city dwellers in that it has made it possible for those people who do not wish to frequent restaurants for one reason or the other, to partake from a variety of items by ordering them in. The latest to jump on the bandwagon is an online delivery service only operating in Karachi that offers its clients free delivery of its cuisine. In fact, so popular have delivery services become that aside from a large number of restaurants now also providing this service for free, a number of businesses have come up for the express purpose of delivering food to consumers at nominal charges from various eateries.

Court Cuisine

Historically, rulers and the nobility have used cuisine as a tool to display their generosity as well as their unique styles of cooking in the royal kitchen. It was customary for rulers to host banquets for nobles and vice versa, and no expenses would be spared in getting lavish menus prepared. The tradition continued, and during the Sultanate and Mughal period rulers regularly organized feasts to entertain their courtiers and foreign guests.

According to Ziauddin Barani, the author of *Tarikh-e-Firuzshahi*, the competition was so great among nobles of the Sultanate to host elaborate feasts that in order to outdo one another in their display of pomp they would often take loans from moneylenders and Multani merchants. Interestingly, a thousand dishes were sometimes served—and that didn't include breads and desserts. Two types of food would be offered at the court—one for the nobility and the other for the commoners.

Later, during the Mughal rule, when rulers and nobles became rich, banquets became even more sophisticated. New dishes, which the Mughals brought from Central Asia, were introduced, and together with Iranian influences on their cuisine another flavour was added to the Mughlai dishes.

However, feasts were held not just for the entertainment of guests, but also, sometimes, to be rid of them! Our history is replete with stories of how rulers would sometimes invite their adversaries to a banquet and then murder them by offering them poisoned dishes!

Street Food

Street food culture goes back to the 1840s when a group of Gujaratis began trading in Bombay's (now Mumbai) Fort area, starting Asia's first stock exchange a few years later. They traded mainly in cotton, and many made fortunes in the period 1861–65 when global supply was affected by the Civil War. These traders worked late into the night when rates were wired in and orders wired out. By the time they would be done, everyone would be hungry but it would be too late for them to eat at home as their kitchens would be closed. So, the traders began to be served by street stalls that invented a late-night special: *pav bhaji*—mashed vegetables (all the leftovers) cooked in tomato gravy and served with buttered loaves. As the city flourished, the food became more varied and included snacks for pleasure rather than just for nourishment. Hence, among others, stalls serving *bhel* (a puffed-rice mixture) and *pani-puri* came up.

However, the gentry would always consider it to be beneath them to eat from wayside stalls, and as for women, it was completely out of the question for them to be seen standing around partaking of street food or even eating while walking on the streets. In fact, eating out was once considered a social taboo. Only travellers, labourers and people who didn't have their family in town were expected to eat at restaurants.

Today, aside from a variety of street stalls, selling anything from *bun kebabs* to *gola gandas* to sweet potatoes to *kachoris*, *haleem*, *chaat*, and a lot more having sprung up practically throughout the country; street food culture is also flourishing in all the major cities and small towns as well, so much so that entire areas have sprung up as food streets. These are now extremely popular, serving a wide variety of fare, and people from all walks of life can be seen frequenting them.

6

Cuisine of Khyber Pakhtunkhwa, FATA, Gilgit-Baltistan, Azad Kashmir

Khyber Pakhtunkhwa

Pashtuns

The frontier Pashtuns generally take two main meals a day, one at forenoon and the other at dinner. Breakfast, if taken, generally comprises a goblet of tea and *roti* or *paratha* fried in *asli ghee* (butterfat), depending on the family's financial status. Eggs, if affordable, are also consumed. *Naan* is baked in a *tandoor*, especially in Peshawar, where traditionally, practically every house has its own *tandoor* and is consumed even for breakfast, or is eaten as large thin *chapatis*, prepared on the *tawa* or on the *tabai*—a special kind of *tawa* intrinsic to many households in Peshawar. This is deeper than the regular *tawa*, has a lid, and the *naan* is baked in it on low heat for a longer period of time than the *chapati*.

Food in Peshawar is closer to the neighbouring Afghanistan's fare—with the ethnic composition of the dominant communities in both areas being the same—than to the Punjabi cuisine. The staple food at lunch and dinner consists of bread made of wheat flour, substituted by *makai ki roti* (corn bread made out of maize flour) on some days, as corn is grown in abundance in the province. Other popular variations of bread include *til walay naan* (sesame seed *naan*); Afghani *roti* (very long and thick *naans*); Peshawari *naan* (stuffed with a mixture of nuts and raisins); *khameeri roti* (bread with yeast); and *gunzakhi* (small *rotis* or rolls prepared with milk, pure fat and *gur*—raw sugar or jaggery). The last is a specialty commonly made in Khyber Pakhtunkhwa when a girl visits her parents' house for the first time after marriage.

Makai ki roti is usually taken with *saag* (indigenous green plants), *lassi* (salted buttermilk) and yogurt, while wheat bread is consumed with cooked vegetables, *daal* or *achar* (pickle). When *khameeri roti* is eaten at dinner, it is a common practice to save at least one, which is kept overnight in the smouldering *tandoor* normally found in every household, and then eaten the following day with the evening tea. So popular is it, that family members normally make a beeline to get to it first.

Fresh water and river fish is popular in the province, especially with the fishermen residing in the Swat region. Local river fish include *rahu* (carp), *mahashair* (tor species), trout and silva. Accompaniments include raw onions and green chillies, though traditionally, the Pashtuns are not in the habit of consuming spicy foods which are more common in central and southern regions of the country. Chilli is consumed mostly in its fresh form and that too, generally by the women folk, green chillies being their favourite. There is, however, liberal use of certain spices in the urban areas of Khyber Pakhtunkhwa.

The poor eat barley or millet—both grown in the region—while dates are often used to supplement food requirements. However, the Pashtuns are very fond of beef and would prefer to partake of it at both meals, if they can afford it. Their fondness for meat is more than amply reflected in the Pushto proverb, which says that even burnt meat is better than pulses. Tribal food is normally cooked in the fat of lamb as most frontier people rear sheep. Infact, unlike in the rest of the country, Pashtuns eat sheep meat as opposed to goat meat. *Turai gosht* (ribbed gourd and meat) is a popular dish. In the absence of meat, milk or milk products and/or vegetables are consumed with bread or rice. Potatoes are the most widely used vegetables. *Gur* is commonly used in the preparation of dishes, as there is an abundance of sugarcane in the area and is normally served at the end of a meal. As with the Pashtuns of Afghanistan, green tea with lots of sugar is popular among the Pashtuns of the area, and is usually taken after meals. When guests are served green tea, the hosts keep refilling their cups until the guests turn their cup over which indicates that they have had enough.

Central to their identity as a Pashtun is adherence to the male-centred code of conduct, *pakhtunwali*. A major dimension of *pakhtunwali* is hospitality or *melmastia*, a trait common among the Pashtuns, whether rich or poor. The Pashtuns serve their guests often beyond their means. They also overspend on food on festive occasions, when goats and sheep are generally slaughtered to celebrate. During the harvesting season, for instance, a farm owner whose land is due for harvesting hosts a special dinner. After the neighbours turn up in large numbers and help their fellow farmer, the family of the landowner serves them meat or chicken *yakhni* (soup) with *naan* broken into pieces. The guests sit around large earthenware bowls in groups of fours and fives and eat directly out of the pot. A complex etiquette surrounds the serving of guests, in which the host and his sons refuse to sit with those they entertain, as a mark of courtesy.

Closely related to *melmastia* is another code of *pukhtunwali*: that of providing refuge to whoever seeks it within the precincts of one's home, even if it is an enemy. For the host, it is a matter of honour to be serving his guests, regardless of who they may be.

Pashtun Specialties

Maize bread — This crispy *roti* comprises lightly fried bread made with maize, *gandana* (leek), spring onions and fresh green chillies kneaded into dough.

Kebab — The kebab has been an evolving term. Although the dish has been native to the Near East and East Mediterranean—especially Greece—since ancient times, it is believed that the first kebab introduced to our part of the world was during the times of Changez Khan, when the horseback riders would kill an animal; clean it; cut it into pieces; thread the pieces over their daggers or swords and cook it over open fire. However, in the fourteenth-century dictionary *Lisan al-Arab*, kebab is defined to be synonymous with *tabahajah*; a Persian word for a dish of fried meat pieces. Persian, in the olden days, was considered to be a more sophisticated language; hence, kebab was used infrequently in Arabic books of that time. Then in the Turkish period, with the appearance of the phrase *sheesh kebab* (skewer with grilled meat), kebab gained its current meaning, whereas, earlier *shiwa* had been the Arabic word for grilled meat. With time kebab has evolved from whole muscle meats to minced meats, and even non-meats.

Chapli Kebabs

Kebabs in Khyber Pakhtunkhwa and Balochistan tend to be identical to the style of barbecue popular in neighbouring Afghanistan, with salt and coriander being the only seasoning used. Beef is generally the most preferred form of meat in Khyber Pakhtunkhwa. In other provinces, kebabs are seasoned with various masalas and tend to be spicy.

Chapli kebab — A gift from the dry fruit traders from Afghanistan who used to cross the Khyber Pass for trade, *chapli kebabs* are round, fatty, minced beef patties fried in *ghee* or animal fat called *dull* in local Pushto. Generous use of onions and tomatoes and in many cases eggs is the norm in *chapli kebabs*, which are spiced with *anardana* (pomegranate seed) and roasted coriander.

Chapal kebab — A cousin of the more common *chapli kebab*, what sets it apart is that it is often tenderized with *maghaz* (brain) and marrow, and seasoned with *mewa* (dry fruits) for added richness.

Lamb tikka/namkeen tikka — Introduced by the Turks, *tikkas* are lamb pieces also prepared over *seekhs*. As in the case of kebabs, the use of spices other than salt is negligible in the *tikkas* eaten in Khyber Pakhtunkhwa. In fact, a variety of *tikka*—mostly served as a starter, known locally as *patay tikka* (concealed tikka)—is made of liver pieces wrapped in fat, cooked over coals only with salt.

Shola/khichri — Sticky rice made with green moong pulses, spices, tomatoes, onions and chunks of beef or mutton, shola is cooked in pure butter fat till it becomes a thick paste. It is served on special occasions, in accompaniment with brown onions and clarified butter.

Yakhni — This is a special broth made from the mince of a lamb's tail, and is popular among the locals of Landikotal.

Sufaid gosht —This meat dish is gently poached using the *dum* process of cooking so common in Central Asia. It is a yogurt-based spiced curry, thus its name which means 'white meat'.

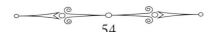

Karhai Namak Mandi — While *karhai* is a popular dish throughout the country the one made in Namak Mandi in Peshawar stands apart. Representing the traditional food of the Afridis—a Pashtun tribe which many historians believe inhabited this terrain even during prehistoric times, while others think they are descended from the Jews, and still others feel they are the original inhabitants of the Gandhara area (Khan 2008). *Karahi Namak Mandi* comprises lamb pieces tossed with fat, salt and ginger. Unlike its counterpart made in other parts of the country, no tomatoes are added to this dish. It is usually eaten with long *kandahari naan.*

Chicken karahi — Inspired by the *balti gosht* of Baltistan, this dish comprises chicken cooked in tomatoes with minimal spices. It gets its name from the wok-like, heavy pan in which it is cooked.

Variety of greens cooked with garlic — The green vegetables grown in Khyber Pakhtunkhwa are different from those found in other parts of the country, and hence some of the vegetarian dishes popular here are peculiar to only this region. *Kachaloo key patton ka saag* made with yam leaves in sesame seed oil; *panerak* (from the malvaceae family), *tara meera saag* (wild water cress), *pishtaray* and *tawa* potato peels, are just some of the unusual greens that are popular in Khyber Pakhtunkhwa.

Talay huey chuzay — Mostly served at breakfast these are young chicks that are fried in green masala and served with honey and *makai ki roti.*

Desserts

Nashasta ka meetha — This sweet dish is made by soaking wheat for a fortnight in water that is changed daily. It is then mashed into a thick paste. This paste is left to dry in the sun for several days until it turns into a powder, after which it is fried in *ghee*. It is especially served to mothers of newborns for forty days after their delivery as it is regarded to enhance lactation. It is also believed to be a cooling agent and is added to sherbets in summer time.

Masalaydar gur — This is jaggery mixed with black pepper, ginger and coconut and served at the end of a meal. It is often presented as gift.

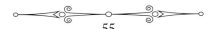

Meethay chawal — Made with rice and *gur* it is served white, unlike the yellow *zarda* served everywhere else in Pakistan. At weddings, it is served with apricot chutney as this fruit grows in abundance there.

Suji ka makhdi halwa — Pudding made with semolina, milk and sugar, this dessert is traditionally made on Shab-e-Barat (All Souls Day) in most households.

Darbesh — Made with semolina, jaggery and crushed dry fruits, these are cooked and set in a tray, and cut into squares before serving.

Beverages

Kachi lassi — Unlike the lassi commonly consumed in the Punjab and Sindh, *kachi lassi* is neither sweet nor salty; it is simply a combination of fresh yogurt and water.

Suji ka Halwa

Special-Occasion Dishes

Weddings

Wedding delicacies include especially prepared loaves of wheat flour or maize called *naghan* baked by village women for marriage feasts. Every loaf has a circumference of about three or four feet and is very thin. The loaves are heaped up in a huge pile in a *karahi* (a wok) and then soaked in soup. Later, *ghee* is poured over them. As many persons as possible sit around the *karahi* and dine out of it. When the first group has finished eating, they are replaced with another group of the same number. Loaves, soup or *ghee* are replenished when the need arises, without cleaning the *karahi*. This continues till all the guests are fed. Meat is also served during such feasts.

Kataway — This is a beef curry dish that is especially served at weddings. It is made with large pieces of meat that are cooked slowly overnight, resulting in the meat becoming extremely tender.

Bannuchi Specialties

There are certain specialties that are associated with the Bannuchis. Concentrated in Bannu district of Khyber Pakhtunkhwa, Bannuchis are mostly farmers and eat whatever staples they grow—maize, barley, millet or wheat—supplemented with buttermilk, *ghee*, *daals* or herbs. Their specialties include:

Sohbat/painda — *Sohbat*, a popular Pashtun dish—especially in Bannu where it is known as *painda*—was initiated by Pashtun men who used to go hunting. It was made by cooking the meat from the hunt into a curry and mixing it with extremely thin, huge *rotis* made over hot stones and shredded into strips. It was normally eaten in a big *thaal* around which all the hunters sat and ate. Today, *sohbat* is made from chicken and the *rotis* are made on regular *tawas*.

Bannu kebab — Deriving its name from the town of Bannu, the *Bannu kebab* is made of lamb *pasanda* (lean meat fillet from thigh portion), incorporating very few spices. A translucent layer of fat, almost like a veil, stays over the meat.

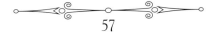

57

Hindkowans

For the Hindkowans, while their food is similar to that eaten in the rest of the Khyber Pakhtunkhwa province, the stress is more on *saags* and *daals* rather than on meat-based dishes. Depending on the availability, *rotis* made with *jowar* (sorghum) or *gehon* (wheat) are eaten, while traditionally only *makai ki rotis* were popular. Their special bread is called *maani* which is wheat *roti* made with egg and milk, similar to a thin pancake. Depending on preference it can be made sweet, or saltish.

A special Hindkowan dessert is *boli* which is made specifically with milk of a buffalo on the third day after it has given birth. It is a kind of custard which only contains sugar, cardamoms and almonds as its added ingredients.

There are several dishes that are in particular prepared for special occasions by Hindkowans:

Post-Wedding — When a Hindkowan bride returns to her maternal home the first time after marriage, the entire family gets together to make *pakwan*, a sweet flour preparation made with eggs and milk, thoroughly kneaded and deep fried. The bride takes these with her for all her in-laws when she returns to her new home. It is taken with tea in the evenings. Another post-wedding speciality is red rice/semolina *rotis*. These are thick, sweet *rotis* cooked in clarified butter and served with dry fruits. This preparation is also made in the bride's maternal home and taken by her for her in-laws.

Ramazan — *Ghee* is taken on a daily basis at *sehri*—meal taken before *fajar* [morning] prayers—with *daal* or *qeema*. It is eaten with *roti* or *paratha*. *Chapli kebab* is eaten at every *iftar*—evening meal to break the fast.

Afghan Refugees

The cuisine of the refugees from Afghanistan, like that of the Pashtuns, is neither too spicy nor too pungent, and yet, is not bland in taste. The peculiarity of this cuisine is its unusual predilection for using animal fat, so much so that even barbecued meat is accompanied

Kabuli Pulao

with fat pieces. Afghans are as famous for their hospitality as the Pashtuns of Khyber Pakhtunkhwa, and it is unthinkable that a visitor would be turned away hungry from their doorstep. They drink green tea practically throughout the day, accompanied by *gur*.

Afghan Specialties

Kabuli pulao — A dish of Middle Eastern/Central Asian origin, *pulao* or 'palav' is often considered to be one of the oldest preparations of rice which has Persian roots. In fact, Persian culinary terms referring to rice preparations are numerous and have found their way into the neighbouring languages. It is a rice and lentil dish in which the rice is cooked in seasoned broth and then brewed. It was known to have been served to Alexander the Great upon his capture of modern Samarkand. Alexander's army brought it back to Macedonia and spread it throughout Eastern Europe. *Kabuli pulao*, which has come to be regarded as the national dish of Afghanistan and has made its way to Khyber Pakhtunkhwa, is made with chopped nuts like pistachios and almonds, and dried orange peels, and topped with fried sliced carrots and raisins. The dish could be made with lamb, chicken or beef. It is served to special guests and on important occasions like weddings.

Ashak — Basically an Afghani dish that has become very popular in Khyber Pakhtunkhwa as well, it is made of *gandana* greens that are boiled, drained and re-boiled several times before being stuffed in flour wrappers folded into triangles (like those used for samosay in other parts of the country), steamed or re-boiled, and served with yogurt.

Sabzi chalow — This is a boiled rice dish and is usually served with mushrooms and spinach.

Beverages

Dogh — A cooling drink especially popular in summer, it is similar to the *lassi* that is consumed in other parts of the country. It incorporates yogurt, salt, dried mint, cucumber and cold water.

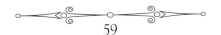

Khows

The main crops of Chitral are barley, wheat and millet, followed by rice, vegetables, fruit, and pulses if the land is arid, hence, the diet of the Khows revolves around these basic ingredients. Although Khow diet is simple, focusing on dairy products and wheat, especially different types of breads, it is rich in variety. Lunch meals generally comprise bread and tea, while rice is consumed for dinner with vegetables, and occasionally meat.

Breads

Khasta shapik — Chitrali yeast bread, *khasta shapik* is thin, round, soft bread cooked on an iron pan. A variation is known as *ishlak/bar shapik/phulka*. Another variation, *chira shapik* is made by boiling milk till it becomes thick, and then layering it between two *phulkas*. *Ghee* is put on the *phulkas* before eating it.

Chapoti — These are thick, round bread cooked on an iron pan and then broiled in the fire-place.

Phoshpaki — This is another popular variation of yeast bread.

Tawa tiki — This cake-like, thick bread made with two *shapiks* placed one on top of the other has a filling inside it, be it of vegetables, meat or any leftovers, and is deep fried. The *tikis* have different names depending on the kind of filling they have. Variations of *tiki* include *mishtiki/chai tiki, sanabach tiki* (with a paste of wheat flour), *pushur tiki* (with a meat filling), *zholai tiki* (with crushed walnuts and onions), and *phinak tiki* (with walnuts and cottage cheese).

Ghalmandi — Comprising two *phulkas* with cheese sandwiched between them, *ghalmandi* is eaten with *ghee* poured on it. A variation is *khista ghalmandi*, which is basically two *khista shapiks* with cheese filling between them and ghee poured on top.

Khow Specialties

Sanabachi — A popular dish, especially cooked during Phindik festival, when livestock is taken for grazing to higher pastures, it comprises a paste of wheat flour cooked in *ghee*.

Lazhek — This is crushed wheat which is cooked with meat and eaten with a spoon. It is generally served on the fourth day following a death to formally denote the end of the mourning period.

Mul — A thin paste of wheat flour, it is cooked in an iron or earthen pot and eaten with *ghee*, milk or cream.

Loganu — This is a soup made with tiny balls of pulse flour boiled in water and then mixed in a broth made from *ghee*, onions, tomatoes, red pepper, and milk or water leftover from the preparation of cheese. Meat can also be added to the soup. A variation made with wheat is called *chira leganu*, while *rishiki* is wheat balls boiled in milk.

Kali — *Kali* is a soup prepared like *loganu* but instead of flour balls, pieces of bread are boiled in water before mixing them with the rest of the ingredients. A variation is *chhira kali* or *sonak* which is similar to *kali* except that it is cooked in milk.

Mulidah — These are pieces of *phulkas* cooked in milk.

Shetu — This is a thin, watery yogurt-like drink.

Shupinak — A delicious thick, creamy cheese, it is made from yogurt.

Desserts

Shoshp — A simple sweet dish, it is made with wheat flour, water and germinated wheat powder cooked in *ghee*, walnut or apricot oil. It is especially prepared on Navroz, a festival to mark the advent of spring.

Kalash

Spread over three valleys in the Chitral region, the Kalash have a distinct lifestyle that is reflected in their cuisine as well. Their ancestry is enveloped in mystery and is the subject of much controversy. They grow wheat which constitutes their staple diet. Their cuisine, like that of the Khows, consists mainly of soups and breads of various kinds. Bread made of corn, and soup made of tomatoes, onions, potatoes and other vegetables are popular. However, if

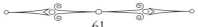

they cannot afford to eat bread in winter, they stock on fruits in the summer right up till autumn to meet their winter requirements. Dried mulberries, apricots and their kernels, and walnuts are eaten during winter.

Kalash sacrifice goats, although, they are not primarily meat-eaters. They only eat it at festivals or when it is sacrificed. Billy-goats are eaten only by men; however, women may eat the meat if it has been slaughtered in the kosher way during funerals or at other major festivals. A sort of porridge is made with meat soup and wheat flour. Goat cheese is an essential protein source produced in the summer, though most of the cheese is eaten by men (Ole Bruun and Arne Kalland). Beans are an important source of protein. A number of festivals are held all through the year, connected one way or the other to the crops sown or harvested. Like in other parts of Pakistan, food plays a major role at these events.

Eggs and chicken are regarded as forbidden foods by the Kalash although with time, these taboos have broken to an extent. They consider onions to be a blessing sent from the heavens. Local wine is prepared during autumn. Milk tea and butter milk are also consumed.

FATA

In the FATA region, the Pashtuns of the frontier and the Afghan refugees that dominate the area, along with maintaining their livestock, primarily grow their own wheat, maize, vegetables and fruits. Their meals comprise large *rotis* made from wheat or maize flour (known in the tribal areas as *jawar*) generally baked in *tandoors* which are in practically every home, or cooked on the *tawa*, eaten with *daals* or vegetables or their favoured meat dishes. Yeast is an essential ingredient in these large *tandoori rotis*. The vegetables eaten are those that are grown in their fertile fields, such as cauliflower, okra, pumpkin, *kachaloo* (yams—even its leaves are cooked as a *saag*), spinach and mustard greens. However, even though the vegetables are the same as in other parts of the country, the method of cooking them in this region is completely different. While vegetables in other parts of Pakistan are generally cooked with *masalas* (spices), adopting the *bhoonoing* technique, the cooked veggies in FATA employ minimum spices—minimal red chillies and coriander—and are stir-fried on the *tawa*. Fruits, lassi and butter are popular accompaniments at meals.

A hospitable people, it is said that in the tribal areas a Pashtun's *dastarkhwan* must have a minimum of three items—rice, chicken and mutton or beef—if they have guests for a meal. The quantity of food is always generous, so that there is food enough to feed many more than the number of guests.

Some of their meat specialties are:

Pattay Tikkay — This is a meat dish heavily laced with fat.

Seena Khwakha — A meat dish, it is first boiled and then cooked in *ghee* using minimum spices.

Paenda — This rice dish is made with the rice arranged like a bowl, and with clarified butter placed in its centre.

Gilgit-Baltistan

Balti

The Balti of Baltistan — sometimes referred to as 'Little Tibet' — use similar spices and ingredients in their cuisine to those used in other Pakistani dishes, such as Mughlai. There is often a base of garlic, ginger, and onion, while the spices used include coriander and cumin, as well as fragrant spices such as star anise, cardamom, clove, and saffron which originate in neighbouring China and Iran. But while Balti cuisine employs similar flavours to other Pakistani and Central Asian cuisines, owing to its unique fusion of influences from the surrounding cultures of Iran, China, Kashmir, Tibet, and Afghanistan; it is distinct in its method. The techniques resemble Chinese wok-cooking, involving stir-fries of pre-cut ingredients, though there are also slow-cooked dishes. In this it resembles its next door neighbour, Tibet, which also fuses subcontinental and Chinese influences in its cuisine. While most Balti dishes are drier, some do have gravies similar to Indian food. Traditionally,

Balti Gosht

pieces of *naan* or other flatbread are used to scoop up food directly from the pot in which it is cooked, while it is still sizzling, rather than serving the food in plates.

The pot is a wok-like vessel known as a *karahi* in other parts of Pakistan but called *balti* (bucket) in Baltistan and in many other cultures in the Himalayan regions. In fact, according to Pat Chapman, author of *Curry Club Balti Curry Cookbook,* it may be possible that the term *balti* for the pot came from the Balti people's use of this particular pot in their cooking. Its concave shape concentrates the heat, just like a wok does, allowing fast cooking without using a lot of wood. Chapman states in his book:

> The origins of Balti cooking are wide-ranging and owe as much to China (with a slight resemblance to the spicy cooking of Szechuan cuisine) and Tibet as well as to the ancestry of the Mirpuris, the tastes of the Moghul emperors, the aromatic spices of Kashmir, and the 'winter foods' of lands high in the mountains.

In the summer months when it is possible to grow vegetables, Balti eat whole-wheat *rotis* cooked slowly on *tawas* and re-cooked over fire, with whatever vegetable that is easily available. In the winter months, however, when there is no growth of vegetables, the diet comprises fruits, spaghetti, *daals* and wheat-based items eaten with *shorba* (soup). Kashmiri tea is a popular beverage that is consumed at least twice a day.

Balti Specialties

Balti Gosht — This meat-based dish is cooked with oil, turmeric, green chillies and salt. No other spices are added to the dish.

Momo — Tibetan in origin, these are flour dumplings that are made with ground meat filling. The meat is cooked with onions, soya sauce, garlic, ginger and cilantro. The dough is rolled out into circles, the filling placed in the centre, and then folded, normally into half-moon shape. The *momos* are then steamed and ready to eat with sauces.

Prabhu — A highly popular dish, these are boiled dumplings made from whole-wheat or barley and eaten with mint and coriander chutney.

Sha balep — Also Tibetan in origin this is bread stuffed with beef.

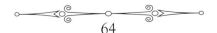

Khobani ka Meetha
(Apricot Dessert)

Desserts

With apricots growing abundantly in the region, a variety of apricot-based desserts are consumed. Popular ways of making *khobani ka meetha* (apricot dessert) are like a *halwa*, or like a *gulab jaman,* except that instead of frying them in *chasni* (sugar water) they are soaked in water overnight and cooked in the same water. Yet another method requires the cooking of the apricots in lots of water until the apricots are softened, and seeds removed. Wheat flour is then added to the mixture and boiled till the mixture acquires a custard-like consistency.

Beverages

Po cha — A typical Tibetan drink, this is butter tea which is consumed all day long by the people to sustain them and keep warm. It is made with cooked tea leaves churned with salt, baking soda (optional), yak butter and goat milk.

Special-Occasion Dishes

Marzan — *Mar* means oil, while *zan* means food, so *marzan* literally means 'food with oil'. This dish is normally cooked at weddings and funerals, and is made with wheat flour that has been boiled in water for fifteen minutes and then pounded into dough with two wooden ladles. The cooked dough is then eaten with *shorba* or soup.

Hunzakutz

Hunzakutz, as the people living in Hunza are known, are believed to have descended from five wandering soldiers of Alexander's army; their fair skin and coloured eyes lending credence to the legend. Regarded as people who do not age—a myth probably perpetuated by the fact that National Geographic magazine selected Hunza as a kingdom where people lived the longest—Hunzakutz grow maize, wheat, barley, millet, fruits including apricots, apples, peaches, pears, pomegranates, certain vegetables and walnuts. Hence, most of their dishes incorporate one or more of these ingredients.

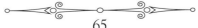

In northern Pakistan, in the high valley of Hunza, food availability has undergone a substantial change in the last five or six decades. Access to Hunza valley, which lies in the heart of the Karakoram Mountains (Western Himalayas) was quite difficult for a long time. But the completion in 1978 of the international Karakoram Highway became a turning point for Hunza. Traversing the valley, the highway became a thoroughfare between Islamabad and Beijing, opening up Hunza to a variety of extraordinary changes. While earlier, rice, chutneys, curries, processed sweets and other delectables were rare in the area, now they are commonplace in local bazaars, and global consumer products are a part of everyday life for the younger generation. Nonetheless, the lifestyles of the scattered mountain tribes have not undergone any radical changes over the years and they continue to grow fruits as their staple food. Hunzakutz have an especially high intake of apricots—which is perhaps, the secret to their long and healthy lives. In the summer months, in order to conserve fuel and precious cereals, cooking is forbidden; hence, the Hunzakutz eat nothing other than apricots. In winter, they eat bread made from apricot kernel flour, and drink brandy made from distilled mulberries and wines from the grapes that grow everywhere. They also consume milk products such as buttermilk, yogurt, butter and cheese.

However, the Hunzakuts do have time-honoured, traditional dishes, which although now largely relegated to community celebrations, are still made by households where the elders call the shots. Some of the dishes even have folktales attached to them—for instance— *diram phitti*, a sweet bread which is made from germinated wheat flour, is connected to a folktale about the seed of life. However, the elders feel that even these traditional dishes made today have a different taste from their original versions as the salt sold in the bazaar, either granulated or as hunks of rock, has a different flavour from the salt from local sources. Also, flour formerly ground at a local water-mill had a different texture from the flour now produced by an electric mill, and this is different again from flour imported from China.

For the elders, the *bokhari* (steel oven) has itself been an innovation, for they had learned to cook at the *shee* (hearth), using stone pots, when there was no *shuli* (stovepipe) to remove smoke from the single-room farmhouse. All of them know the difference in taste between *phitti* baked in a *tandoor* of sorts, and *phitti* baked in an electric oven.

Breads

Diram phitti — It is believed that one of the Mirs of Hunza was warned of a conspiracy against his life from within his own ranks. He was told that the Diramiting tribe would take over his realm and that his only protection would be to slay every single male member of that tribe. So the Mir ordered this by decree. But as soon as this decree was executed, all crops became infected, threatening famine. Mir's only hope for salvation was to find a male Diramiting survivor; seeds sown from whose hands would secure the Mir's redemption and rid the crops of disease. This he did, and kept his promise to protect the seed of the Diramiting, thereby, ensuring that life returned back to Hunza soil. *Diram phitti*, a form of sweet bread made from wheat flour, is symbolic of this legend.

Phitti — Probably the most famous of all Hunza breads, this whole-wheat flour bread is a common breakfast food. Thick and nutritious, it is crusty from the outside and soft from the inside, and is time consuming to prepare. The dough is put into a sealed metal container and the *phitti* is baked overnight over the embers of the hearth.

Hunzakutz Specialties

Maltash — Aged butter prepared from milk that is scalded before churning, its strong taste is so valued that it is often given as a gift at births, weddings and funerals. The older the *maltash*, the more valuable it is. Wrapped in birch bark and buried in the ground it may lay there for years or even decades before the head of the family decides it is time to dig it out.

Girgir aloo — This dish is a combination of whole *masoor ki daal* and potatoes, cooked with tomatoes, onions and spices.

Doudo — Soup cooked with home-made noodles and vegetables such as potatoes and spinach, it is thickened with whole-wheat flour and eggs. It comes in many varieties such as *kurutze duodo* with *kurutz*, and the delicious *haneetze doudo* with nuts or crushed apricot kernels, garlic and onion. Since apricots grow in abundance in Hunza, apricot soup made with dried apricots, flour and water is also popular.

Kurutz — A salty, sour, rock-hard, home-made goat cheese, it is eaten both on its own, and as a flavouring in a soup. It is made by condensing buttermilk, pressing it, and then sun-drying it. Cheese is made using a similar method, all the way from Mongolia to Tibet.

Burusshapik — *Burus* is a soft, home-made goat cheese, and *burusshapik* is *burus* cooked into a whole-wheat *chapati*, its outside covered in apricot-kernel oil. It is served cold, and is very filling.

Burus berikutz — Similar to *burusshapik*, the bread is also layered with herbs such as coriander and mint, and served in small pieces.

Chapshuro — A kind of pizza, it is made of meat, onions and tomatoes cooked into a thick *chapati*. Sometimes these ingredients are sandwiched between two *chapatis* and fried.

Khamuloot pie — This is a thick bread, almost like a pie, mixed with onion and meat and cooked on wood fire.

Beverages

Tumuro — A tea brewed from a wild alpine herb similar to sage, called *tumuro*, this drink is said to cool and clear the head, especially at high elevation.

Hunza water — Deceptively called Hunza water, this is a home-made mulberry wine that is served to all guests—in spite of the Islamic prohibition on liquor—by some Hunzakutz, and is famous for bestowing long life and youth to its consumers.

Diltar — Similar to *lassi* consumed practically throughout Pakistan, this yogurt drink is traditionally prepared in goat or sheep skin which is vigorously shaken or rolled on the ground till butter is formed.

Mughals

The name Mughal is derived from the original homelands of the Timurids, the Central Asian steppes once conquered by Changez Khan, and so known as Moghulistan, 'Land of Mongols'. Although early Mughals maintained Turko-Mongol practices, they were heavily

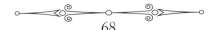

influenced by Persian culture, forming the base for Indo-Persian culture, and giving birth to a cuisine using indigenous spices and ingredients but strongly influenced by Persian and Turkic cuisines of Central Asia.

The taste of Mughlai cuisine varies from extremely mild to spicy, and is often associated with a distinctive aroma and the flavour of ground and whole spices. The Mughlai dishes that have become popular in Pakistan are consumed in practically all the major cities of Pakistan. Menus at lavish spreads could include rich, spicy curry dishes such as *qorma* and *koftas* (balls of minced or ground meat), and rice dishes such as *biryani* and *zerda* not to mention *murgh musslam*, and *shahi tukray* for dessert. For the purpose of this book, the dishes have mostly been covered in conjunction with the community that has come to be most associated with it. However, there are some universal favourites that are listed below:

Mughlai Specialties

Qorma — This is a characteristically creamy and silky Persian-Indian dish the origin of which can be traced to Kashmir, from where it made its way to the Mughal courts, where it was adapted to its present form. *Qorma* is generally a mild curry made with chicken, beef or lamb and only a few vegetables, such as onions and potatoes. The flavour is based on a mixture of spices, including ground coriander and cumin, combined with yogurt kept below curdling temperature, and incorporated slowly and carefully.

Biryani — *Biryani* comes from the word *Birian* which means 'fried before cooking' in Persian. The dish was later adopted by the Mughal emperors who found this a convenient meal to serve their soldiers as it contained all essential nourishments rolled into one delicious dish. Legend has it that it was introduced by the Turkic chieftain *Timur*, who brought the recipe with him from Central Asia, while yet another belief is that it was introduced to the subcontinent by Arab traders. Lizzie Collingham in her book *Curry: A Tale of Cooks and Conquerors*, states that the third Mughal emperor, Akbar was responsible for the 'process of synthesis' that also 'went on in the kitchens' and that it was in his time that the 'delicately flavoured Persian pulao met the pungent and spicy rice dishes of Hindustan to create the classic Mughlai dish, *biryani*'. Yet another belief is that empress

Chicken Reshmi Kebab   *Murgh Mussalam*

Mumtaz Mahal had discovered this recipe and ordered it to be prepared for the armies of her husband, Shah Jahan. Whichever the case may be, *biryani* became so popular during the Mughal period, that it was widely adopted by other communities — with slight changes, of course — so that all claim ownership of this delicious dish. It is believed that there are at least twenty-six different varieties of *biryani* in vogue these days.

Today *biryani* has become a loosely used term for a rice dish generally cooked with fried meat or vegetables using the *dum* technique of cooking. The rice is boiled separately and arranged on top of the cooked meat, which has been marinated in browned onions, yogurt, and whole *garam masala*. The rice is then sprinkled with saffron-infused milk and the pot is tightly sealed and cooked very slowly, using the *dum* technique. The end result is an intensely aromatic dish, served in accompaniment with *raita* or *kachumar*. *Biryani* is one of the few special-occasion dishes that are served as frequently at weddings as at funerals, and as much at parties as at home for family consumption.

Murgh mussalam — A special dish of Persian origin, this is a classic royal dish basically comprising stuffed chicken in a creamy sauce. The spices are fried or dry-roasted, ground into a paste made rich with cashew nuts, almonds and raisins, and stuffed into the chicken. It is generally simmered in milk and then finally thickened with natural yogurt.

Reshmi kebab — This traditional Mughlai dish derives its name from the texture of the meat (*reshmi* meaning silken) after prolonged marinating and light braising. It is a classic ground meat kebab, bound with eggs and cooked on skewers over charcoal.

Daal makhni — Made with lots of butter and cream, traditionally this *daal* was cooked over charcoals on low flame for hours, giving it a creamy texture. When cooked at home these days, more moderate amounts of cream or butter are used. Lentils and beans have to be soaked overnight for at least eight hours and gently simmered on low heat along with ginger, garlic and *garam masala*. These are then combined with a tangy masala base which includes onions, tomatoes, dried mango powder and sometimes pomegranate seeds.

Pasanday

Chicken makhni — A rich man's variation, this delectable dish is made with chicken pieces cooked in butter, tomatoes, yogurt and masala.

Pasanda — Served in the court of the Mughal emperors, *pasandas*—a variation of the word *pasand* meaning 'fond of'—refers to the prime cut of meat used in the preparation of this dish. Originally made with leg of lamb flattened into strips, and marinated and fried in yogurt and spices, these thin steaks are now generally made of beef.

Do pyaza — The name of the dish literally means 'two onions'—onions are added at two stages of the cooking process, hence the name. It is made with meat, chicken or prawns, but could also be purely vegetarian. According to one legend, this dish is a specimen of a particular gourmand's ingenuity. The gourmand was a mullah (preacher) and one of the famed 'nine jewels' in the court of Akbar the Great (the renowned Mughal emperor of India in the latter half of the sixteenth century). He maintained an open house, so that a steady stream of guests would arrive all evening, often many more than were expected. When he would realize that the food would not be sufficient for all those who had dropped by, he would clap loudly to indicate to the cook that more onions should be added to the meat to make it last longer. He discovered that doubling the quantity of onions made the dish even tastier.

According to another legend, this dish was named after a minister of Emperor Akbar, named Mullah Do-Pyaza. The dish evolved further in Hyderabad and became a Hyderabadi specialty.

Desserts

Shahi tukray — A legacy of the Mughals, this delicious bright yellow coloured dessert which literally means 'royal pieces' is made with fried bread slices cooked in milk with sugar and saffron, and garnished with slivers of almonds and pistachios.

Jalebis — Persian in origin—it is known as *zulbiya* in Persian. Legend has it that the Mughal emperor Jehangir introduced *jalebis* to the subcontinent. This crispy sweet treat has a spiral shape and is made of flour doused in sugar syrup. Although eaten through the year, it is particularly popular in Ramazan, both at *sehri* and *iftari*.

Mongols

Mongolian cuisine primarily consists of dairy products, meat, and animal fats. Use of vegetables and spices is limited. Due to the geographic proximity and deep historic ties with China and Russia, Mongolian cuisine is also influenced by Chinese and Russian cuisine. Meat is cooked; used as an ingredient for soups or dumplings; or dried for winter. Milk and cream are used to make a variety of beverages, as well as cheese and similar products.

Mongolian Specialties

Buuz — Served as an appetizer, these steamed dumplings are similar to the Balti *momo*. However variations are also made that are boiled in water (*bansh*), or deep fried in mutton fat (*khuushuur*).

Tajiks

Tajiks are a Persian-speaking people, with traditional homelands in present-day Afghanistan, Tajikistan, southern Uzbekistan, northern Pakistan and western China. The Pakistani Tajiks are estimated to be over one million. Tajiks of Pakistan are normally considered to be similar to Khows and their cuisine has much in common with Persian, Afghan, and Uzbek cuisines. Traditional Tajik meals begin with a spread of dry fruit, nuts, *halwa* (sweet meats), and other desserts arranged in small dishes; progresses onto soup and meat; and culminates in the serving of *palav*.

Tajik Specialties

Palav/osh — *Palav*, generically known as *plov*, is the national dish in Tajikistan, as in other countries in the region. This particular rice dish is made with shredded yellow turnip or carrot and pieces of meat, all fried together in vegetable oil or mutton fat in a special *qazan* (a wok-shaped cauldron) over an open flame. The meat is cubed, the carrots are chopped finely into long strips, and the rice acquires a yellow or orange hue from frying the carrots. The dish is eaten communally from a single large platter placed at the centre of the table.

Qurutob — Its name connotes the preparatory method of this dish: *qurut* means dried balls of salty cheese while *ob* means water. The balls are dissolved in water and the liquid is poured over strips of thin, flaky flatbread made with butter or tallow for flakiness. Before serving, the dish is topped with onions fried in oil until golden-brown, and other fried vegetables.

Sambusa — These are triangular-shaped very thin pastry stuffed with mince meat and baked in an oven. Fried variations of it known as *samosa* have become popular in the country since the time of the Mughals, with filling ranging from mince meat (mutton, beef or chicken) to vegetables, generally potatoes. Served in most communities as a snack item, it often constitutes a side dish in Muslim Gujarati meals.

Beverage

Green tea — Green tea is the national drink of Tajikistan. Tea accompanies every Tajik meal and is frequently offered between meals as a gesture of hospitality to guests and visitors. It is served hot in a china pot with a lid and is drunk without sugar from small saucer-less mugs.

Azad Kashmir

Kashmiri cuisine has evolved over hundreds of years. The first major influence was the food of the Kashmiri Buddhists and Pandits—the Hindus who lived in the valley in the Middle Ages. Kashmiri cooking developed initially as two great schools of culinary craftsmanship— Kashmiri 'Pandit' and 'Muslim'. While both ate meat, the basic difference between the two was that the Hindus used *heeng* and yogurt in their cuisine, and the Muslims onions and garlic, two ingredients which orthodox Hindus avoided. In the cuisine of the former, no meat delicacy—except certain kebabs—was cooked without yogurt. Even vegetarian dishes often incorporated it.

The cuisine was, subsequently, heavily influenced by later cultures which arrived, beginning with the invasion of Kashmir by Timur in the fifteenth century from what is now Uzbekistan, and the migration of 1700 skilled woodcarvers, weavers, architects, calligraphers and cooks from Samarkand to the valley of Kashmir. The descendants of these cooks, the *wazas*, are the master chefs of Kashmir. Other strong influences included that of Central Asian, Persian, Afghan and Punjabi cultures.

In fact, Kashmiri cuisine today is a unique blend of Indian, Iranian, and Afghani cuisines. It is essentially meat-based—so much so that unlike most Brahmins, Kashmiri Brahmins once living in Azad Kashmir were also non-vegetarian—and centred on a main course of rice. Not surprisingly, Kashmir excels in the preparation of non-vegetarian cuisine and more so in meat-based dishes, with lamb preferred over others. Kashmiris are also liberal in the use of spices, condiments and yogurt. The medium of cooking is chiefly mustard oil. Another characteristic of the Kashmiri cuisine is the generous use of saffron or *kesar*, produced locally.

A local spinach-like green called *haak* is popular in the summer months, as are lotus roots, which are used as a meat substitute. In fact, fresh vegetables are abundant in the summer, including a prized variety of mushrooms called *guhchi*, used only for special occasions. Fresh fish is also favoured in the summer, while smoked meat, dried fish, and sun-dried vegetables are used in the winter. The abundance of dry fruit and nuts (walnuts, dates, and apricots) in the region has inspired their use in desserts, curries, and snacks. Sauces for curries are also made from dairy-rich products.

The ultimate formal banquet in Kashmir now only found in Muzaffarabad is the royal Wazwan brought to the region about five hundred years ago from Central Asia. It is a blend of the culinary styles of the Mughals and Persians who were Muslims; and the Kashmiri Pandits who were Hindu Brahmins. As many as forty courses may be served during Wazwan, with at least 12 and up to 30 courses being non-vegetarian, cooked overnight by the Vasta

Waza (master chef), and his retinue of wazas. Wazwan is regarded as the pride of Kashmiri culture and identity.

Guests are seated in groups of four and share the meal out of a large metal platter called the *trami*. The meal begins with a ritual washing of hands in a basin called the *tash-t-nari*, which is taken round the guests by attendants. Then the *tramis* arrive, heaped with rice, quartered by four *seekh kebabs*, and containing four pieces of *methi qorma*, two *tabak maaz*, *white murgh*, *saffron murgh*, and much more. Yogurt garnished with Kashmiri saffron, salads, Kashmiri pickle and chutney are served separately in small earthen pots. Everytime a *trami* gets polished off, it is removed and replaced by a new one until the dinner runs its course.

Seven dishes that are a must in such banquets, are *rista*, *rogan josh*, *tabak maaz*, *daniwal korma*, *aab gosht*, *marchwangan qorma* and *gushtaba*. Other Kashmiri specialties which could be included in the feast are *Kashmiri gobi*, *Nalagarh eggplant*, and *Narangi pulao*. The former is cauliflower cooked with cashew nuts and cayenne pepper, together with an aromatic tomato sauce. *Nalagarh eggplant* comprises eggplants served in yogurt, while *Narangi pulao* is traditionally served with a layer of fried potatoes and yogurt mixture sandwiched between rice, making it into a wholesome meal. The feast ends with an elder leading the thanksgiving to Allah, which is heard with rapt attention by everyone.

Breads

Baqerkhani — Kashmiri *baqerkhani* has a special place in Kashmiri cuisine. It is believed that it most likely originated in the Middle East and eventually spread to Kashmir. It is similar to a round *naan* in appearance, but crisp and layered, and sprinkled with sesame seeds. Traditionally, *kandurs* or *baqerkhaniwalas* (bread-makers) ignited their *tandoor* ovens around midnight to have the bread available by morning. In order to make the bread, *baqerkhani* dough of white flour and *mewa* is kneaded well and stretched thin by hand over the entire span of a wooden board. It is divided into small portions, and then after spreading *ghee* over it, flour is strewn on; the dough folded; and the process repeated several times. Each dough portion is then rolled out into a *roti* and sesame seeds are spread on it. The *rotis* are then baked in the *tandoor*. During the process of baking, milk may be sprinkled on the dough. Nowadays however, in place of *ghee* and milk, molasses solution is often added so that the colour of the bread turns reddish. The Kashmiri *baqerkhani* is typically consumed hot for breakfast.

Kashmiri Specialties

Shab daigh — This is a beautiful blend of whole or halved turnips, tender mutton pieces or minced mutton shaped into meatballs, *ghee* and little sugar cooked over low heat all night long (hence the word *shab* in the name which means 'night' in Persian). This results in an incredibly rich and flavourful gravy laced with gentle spices, saffron and seasoning. In the early eighteenth century, when the Mughal Empire was on the decline, the glory of Awadh lured Kashmiri families to move to Lucknow, the capital of Awadh, in search of alternate sources of employment (Collingham 2006). They brought with them the scent of saffron and their celestial cuisine. The cooking of *shab daigh* in winter for the Nawab of Awadh became not only a celebration of winter, but a reminder of the bond of the migrant families with their motherland. It was then adopted by Delhi, but with a slight difference. Today, both kinds of *shab daigh* are popular in Pakistan—the one made by Kashmiris which incorporates turnips and also has sugar as one of the ingredients, and the other introduced by Dilliwallay who moved to Pakistan after Partition, which incorporates carrots instead of turnips.

Shab Daigh

Dum Aloo

Mutanjan

Rogan josh — *Rogan* means 'clarified butter' in Persian, while *Josh* means 'hot'. *Rogan josh*, thus, means meat cooked in clarified butter, at intense heat. Adopted by the Kashmiris, this aromatic curry dish comprises lamb cooked generally with yogurt and saffron, and has a deep red colour thanks to a liberal use of Kashmiri dried chillies and the dried flower of the cockscomb plant (*maval*) indigenous to Kashmir, with red flowers. In fact, some historians believe that this red colour gives the dish its name as *rogan* in Kashmiri means 'red' (Collingham 2006). It is made without onions and garlic when prepared by Brahmins (they use fennel and asafoetida instead). However, the version now eaten of *rogan josh* in Pakistan, particularly by Dilliwallay, was popularized by the Mughals who ruled the Indian subcontinent for three centuries. The unrelenting heat of the plains took the Mughals frequently to Kashmir, which is where *rogan josh* was perfected (Collingham 2006). Some preparations of *rogan josh* are very lavish, with lots of sweet spices and liberal amounts of cream.

Mutanjan — Similar to *biryani* eaten in the rest of the country, this sweetish meat and rice dish is made by boiling whole spices and onions placed in a bag, and lamb meat. When cooked, sugar and lemon is added to the meat, and then it is sandwiched between layers of par-boiled rice. The rice is topped with saffron milk and nuts.

Qabargah — Lamb rib chops cooked in a spice mixture, these are then coated in a *besan* batter and fried.

Dum aloo — This potato dish is made with favourite Kashmiri spices like fennel/aniseed and ginger powder. So named because it is cooked in its own juices using the *dum* technique or under pressure, this dish is made by frying potatoes and then simmering them slowly in spices and yogurt. It is eaten with rice.

Tabak maaz — These are flat pieces of mutton cut from the ribs and made with *malai* (whole cream) and saffron. The pieces are fried till they acquire a crisp crackling texture.

Gushtaba — Pounded and spiced meat balls cooked in yogurt and milk sauce, the meat is usually lamb.

Rista — Similar to *gushtaba*, these are small rice balls cooked in tomato curry, but with less spices and meat in the sauce.

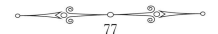

Harissa — This dish comprises beef cooked with green gram into a thick paste. It is served only in winter.

Daniwal qorma — Made with leg of lamb cut into pieces, spices, onions, saffron and yogurt, the trick to cooking this dish lies in cooking the yogurt until it is thickened and reduced to half its quantity, before incorporating the lamb into it.

Aab gosht — *Aab* means water in Persian. Mixed with the flavours of fennel, cardamom, cumin, cinnamon, and black pepper that are placed in a muslin bag and cooked on low heat all night, it makes for a unique lamb chops dish that is cooked in its stock with yogurt and tomatoes.

Marchwangan qorma/mirch qorma — This is basically boiled lamb cooked in spices, to which red chilli and brown onion pastes are added when parboiled. When the meat is almost ready, ginger and fennel powders and dried mint is added to the dish.

Doodh ras lamb — Cooked in milk, this lamb dish comprises boiled lamb that has been cooked with whole spices wrapped in muslin, and then re-cooked in thickened milk.

Methi maaz — Made with boiled meat and fenugreek, and few spices, this dish is also cooked in milk.

Kashmiri Vegetarian Specialties

Hak — This is a stir-fried spinach dish. It used to be very popular at breakfast. Generally eaten with *hak* chutney and butter, this dish is now popular only in traditional homes.

Nadur yakhni — Comprising boiled lotus roots, this dish is made by simmering the boiled lotus in sautéed yogurt.

Nadur palak — A variation of *nadur yakhni*, *nadur palak* (*nadur* are lotus roots and *palak* is spinach) consists of stir-fried lotus roots and spinach.

Razmah goagji — This simple dish is made with boiled turnips and dried beans stir-fried in mustard oil.

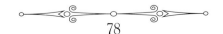

Nun Chai
(Kashmiri Chai)

Beverages

Kashmiri chai (Nun chai) — Pink tea flavoured only with salt (crushed almonds, cocoa and pistachio nuts added to it these days are a later addition), has now become a universal favourite practically all over Pakistan in the winter months. It is served primarily at weddings and formal occasions. Made with black tea, it incorporates milk and bicarbonate of soda, which gives it the pinkish colour. Kashmiris normally have it for breakfast with fresh *baqerkhani*.

Qehwa — An aromatic black tea, most Kashmiris believe—even though its exact origins are still unclear—that *qehwa* dates back to time immemorial and has been a part of local consumption for centuries. Certain sources trace the origins of the drink to the Yarkand valley in Xinjiang area. Some areas of Kashmir and Xinjiang were part of the Kushan Empire during the first and second century AD, and it is likely that the use of *qehwa* and the spread of its popularity in these regions was facilitated during the Kushan rule. In fact, its fame spread to Khyber Pakhtunkhwa, Chitral, and the northern areas to the extent that it is usually served after every meal in these areas. It is flavoured with saffron, cardamom, and almonds and served from a samovar, a large metal kettle originating in the Russian steppes.

7

Punjab

Rich in agricultural land, the Punjab grows wheat, barley, corn and rice among other food grains. Wheat is the staple food grain in affluent Punjabi families, while millet, barley and maize are the staple food of the laity in the rural areas. Rural Punjabis also partake of meals comprising thick *chapatis* made of rice of inferior quality, accompanied by *lassi*, onions and chillies. The farmers in the rural areas consume green grams and vegetables along with the staples. *Sattu*, made of barley seeds is a popular drink in some villages, especially in the summer, and is often taken at lunch, along with *missi roti* made of mixed wheat and gram, flavoured with salt and chillies. In other rural areas of the province, breakfast simply comprises wheat bread or bun taken with buttermilk (incorporating dried whole milk known as *khoya*) in summer; and with milk in winter. *Parathay* made of wheat flour are also popular for breakfast in many homes, often eaten with the previous evening's leftovers or yogurt, along with buttermilk, or fresh cream. The bread is mostly baked in *tandoors*. Often, it is the previous night's leftover bread that is fried in oil and eaten at breakfast.

Another item commonly consumed by the common man in summer, is *achar* made of raw mangoes. It is taken as a substitute for *daal* or curry and is eaten with bread. In winter, the food usually consists of rice, maize, *saag* and *daal*, while okra is a popular vegetable in summer. Other than *saag*, the vegetables in season and popular in winter are turnips, carrots and radish. *Ghee* is an integral part of the diet. Dates also form a major part of the staple diet in some parts of the province.

In southern Punjab which is dominated by Siraikis, the cuisine is much the same as in the rest of the province. Generally, two meals are consumed—breakfast, comprising *parathay* and tea topped with cream—and supper, eaten around four in the evening. While there isn't much difference in the food, there are certain greens, such as *swanjna* that are grown only in the southern belt which are consumed here. Its roots and *phallis* (green beans) are used to make *achar*. *Tandoori roti* is generally made with whole-wheat flour without any refined flour and baking soda added to it, and so is healthier than the *rotis* found in the rest of the province.

In the hilly areas, smoked meat and *kak* (baked balls of wheat flour) are served to guests. In Mianwali, meat fried on burning coal is a specialty. In other towns, families of average income normally take wheat *chapatis*, meat (mostly beef) curry, cooked pulses and vegetables. Boiled rice is occasionally eaten as well, in accompaniment with curry, and is not taken in the form of *chapatis* as in the rural areas. Buttermilk and milk are universally popular accompaniments and the former is also popular at breakfast. Fish is rarely eaten in the summer, but is consumed in winter.

In the Punjab, on marriage occasions especially, guests are usually served rice or wheat *chapatis*. Sweet dishes include *firni* made from cream of rice and milk, *halwa*, *sewayian* (vermicelli) and milk or *malai* (double cream), and *jalebi*.

In Lahore, breakfast tends to be a bit more elaborate in affluent homes, particularly on weekends and public holidays. *Baqerkhani*, *paya* (beef trotters) and yogurt with sugar or buttermilk are popular holiday breakfast items, while toast/rusk with tea is consumed on weekdays. At lunch, *parathay*, which are large puris made of a flour dough mixed with either a pulse or ground meat, are often eaten with *daal*.

Although the fragrant spices used in the north such as saffron, cardamoms and cloves are also used in cooking here, emphasis is placed more on the usage of plants that grow better in the Punjab such as mustard, black pepper, asafoetida, and *kari* leaf (which some say is the source of the Indo-British word, 'curry'). The main ingredients used in Punjabi cuisine though, are basic: onions, ginger, garlic, and *ghee*.

Among the minority groups living in the Punjab are the Sikhs, who must be mentioned here, as unlike the other communities present who are found in greater numbers in other parts of the country, the Sikhs are mostly concentrated in the Punjab. According to the 2008 population census, they roughly number twenty thousand.

Aloo ke Parathay   *Murgh Cholay*

Breads

Stuffed parathay — Stuffed fried *rotis* of white flour, the stuffing varies from mashed potatoes, cauliflower, and turnips to minced meat, onions, and corn.

Katlama — These are delicious fried *parathas* with masala sprinkled on top. They are sold on the wayside on pushcarts.

Punjabi Specialties

Murgh cholay — Chicken cooked with boiled chickpeas, this is a quintessentially Punjabi dish that has recently become popular in other parts of the country as well.

Phaturay/kachori* with *cholay — Regarded as a classic Punjabi dish, *cholay phaturay*, surprisingly enough, originated in Delhi (where it is known as bhaturay) and its surrounding areas. *Phaturay* are soft and fluffy fried *puris* with *maash ki daal* mixed into the dough. They are popular with chickpea curry, *achar* and salad.

Acharee murghi — Made in mustard oil with ground roasted spices, whole spices, onions and tomatoes, this chicken dish has a tangy taste.

Paya/siri paya — Believed to be a dish of Mughal origin *siri paya* or *paya* was considered a delicacy for the Nawabs, as the *siri* (the head) and *paya* (the feet or trotters) were the most expensive parts of the animal. Traditionally, it is a breakfast dish—its preparation a painstaking job. The *siri* and *paya* have to be first roasted over open fire to burn off the hair from the skin while taking care not to scorch the skin since that would spoil the flavour of the dish. The *siri* and *payas* are then cooked for a long time in masalas until the soupy curry acquires a sticky consistency. The sticky soup base is generally created by sautéed onions, tomatoes, and garlic to which a number of curry-based spices are added. In times gone by when people used wood or coal as a cooking fuel, women would cook this dish all night on low heat. It is the prolonged cooking that melts the fat in the *payas* giving the curry a sticky consistency. Payas are usually eaten with *naan* for breakfast in the winters. Fresh chopped coriander, ginger, green chillies and sliced lemon are used as garnish. Recipe for this dish varies slightly from region to region.

Paye cholay — A combination of beef trotters and chickpeas, this dish is eaten mostly in the Punjab.

Lahori fried fish — A batter-coated, spicy fried fish, the Lahori fried fish is generally made with fillet pieces of *rahu*. It is deep fried in a huge *karahi*, and eaten with chutney and finely cut radish.

Lahori Fried Fish

Paye

Taway wali machli — Supposedly introduced by Darul Mahi, a restaurant in Lahore, this dish comprises sweet water fish fried on a *tawa* and seasoned with *chaat ka masala*.

Karalay gosht — This dish is made with bitter gourd that has been cleaned and salted, and then deep fried. It is mixed with meat, generally of the rump, fried onions and spices, and then cooked again. It requires experience to get this dish just right and overcome the bitter taste of the gourd.

Tandoori chicken — One of the widely-known survivors of court cuisine, *tandoori murghi* takes its name from the *tandoor* in which it is cooked. The chicken pieces are first marinated for hours in aromatic spices and yogurt, then threaded into skewers and roasted in the *tandoor*. It is the aroma of the clay oven and charcoal, as well as the spices that makes this chicken dish so unique and tasty.

Gonglu — Also known as *shalgham*, this is a curry dish made with turnips and meat, normally served with white rice. Originally, *gur* was added to the dish at the tail-end of the cooking.

Kunna — A Chiniot (a town in Punjab) speciality, *kunna* is similar to *nihari* made by Dilliwallay except that in the latter, beef is used, whereas, *kunna* is a mutton dish. It is cooked overnight on low heat in a sealed earthen pot.

Sarson ka saag* with *makai ki roti — A combo meal regarded to be very nutritious, *sarson ka saag* and *makai ki roti* is normally eaten in winter. The former comprises mustard green leaves cooked on low heat and mashed to a porridge-like consistency. It is eaten with maize flour bread, shaped by hand. The bread is yellow in colour when ready, and has much less adhesive strength than normal bread, which makes it difficult to handle. Owing to this, making *makai ki roti* is more difficult than making *roti* from wheat flour. Often *lassi* and butter form the accompaniments to this vegetarian meal.

Katakat — Comprising leftover organs of lamb—heart, kidney, liver, testicles—*katakat* is prepared on a large *tawa* by pounding the organs into very tiny pieces—hence its name (*katakat* is the sound that emanates from the pounding).

Seekh kebab aur malai — A quintessentially Rawalpindi favourite, this combination of beef kebabs and full cream is rarely eaten in other parts of the country.

Chargha — A light, tangy-flavoured delicacy, *chargha* is made with whole chicken which is first marinated only with lemon juice and then overnight with other spices as well. It is then deep fried.

Desserts

Churi — Normally eaten at breakfast, it is prepared with ground *roti*, butter and sugar.

Halwa–puri — The word *halwa* originally derived from the Arabic root *halw* (sweet)—is used to describe many distinct types of sweet confection across the Middle East, Central Asia, South Asia, and the Balkans. *Halwas* can take many forms, but the one popularly eaten with *puris* is made of semolina (*suji*).

Panjiri — A classic Punjabi dish made from whole-wheat flour fried lightly in sugar and *ghee*, *panjiri* is heavily laced with dry fruits—in fact, five types of dry fruits cut finely are used, thus the name *panj* meaning five—and herbal gums. It is usually eaten in winter to ward off cold, and given to mothers after their delivery as it is believed to boost the production of breast milk. It is also often presented at weddings from the groom's side, to the bride's family.

Thooti wali kheer — Known as *firni* in other parts of the country, *thooti wali kheer* derives its name from *thooti*, derived from *thoota*, meaning 'thumb'. In the Punjab, as indeed in Sindh, the dessert is served in small, earthenware bowls and often scooped out with the thumb, thus the name.

Bateesa — A crispy-flaky *mithai*, *bateesa* is made with flour, gram flour, sugar, water and milk cooked together and then poured into a *thaali* and rolled to one inch thickness. It is supposed to have 32 fine layers, hence its name *bateesa* (*batees* means 32). When ready, it is cooled and cut into squares.

Lassi

Gajar ka halwa/gajrella — This dessert is a winter favourite, when carrots are in full season. It is made with freshly grated carrots, milk and sugar cooked together, and then fried in ghee. The dish is garnished with slivers of pistachios and almonds.

Fruits on ice — Peculiar only to the Punjab, this wayside favourite sold on pushcarts in the sweltering summer heat comprises fruits that have been chilled over slabs of ice, and seasoned with masala.

Gola ganda — An assortment of coloured syrups poured over crushed ice, often topped with condensed milk, this is also a wayside favourite particularly in summer months.

Mewawalla gur — Made of dry fruits and *desi ghee* (clarified butterfat), this is a soft *mithai*, eaten all year round.

Alsi ki pinya — These are rock-hard balls made from linseed, sugar and *desi ghee*, and are eaten in winter months.

Pura — Similar to a pancake, it is made out of whole-wheat flour.

Punjabi Snacks

Samosa cholay — Peculiar to the Punjab, this is a *chaat* dish that is an amalgamation of a potato *samosa* broken down into bite-size pieces and topped with *chana chaat*.

Punjabi Beverages

Lassi — A refreshing drink, *lassi* is made with yogurt, milk and sugar. Sometimes sugar is replaced by salt.

Peray wali lassi — A richer version of the normal *lassi*, this refreshing drink is made by pounding *khoya* and pouring it into a glass of *lassi* and then topping it with beaten milk till a thick layer of butter appears.

Doodh khoya — Another rich drink, it is made with caramelized milk and has a thick layer of *tukham-i-balanga* (basil seeds) and dry fruit on top.

Doodh patti — Very popular, especially at roadside cafes, *doodh patti* is tea cooked in milk.

Sikanjbeen — A great favourite in summer, this ice-cold drink is made with lime juice, sugar, salt and black pepper.

***Falooda* sundae** — *Falooda* is thought to be an adaptation of the Persian dessert *faloodeh*, brought to the surrounding Middle Eastern countries and South Asia by Muslim travellers and merchants. *Falooda* is a popular summer drink throughout Pakistan, made primarily by mixing rose syrup with noodles and tapioca seeds along with either milk or water. In addition to these basic ingredients, basil seeds, tutti-fruiti, sugar and ice cream may be added. The rose syrup may be substituted with another flavoured base.

Sattu — Barley drink, it is made with barley that has been cut before it is fully matured, and roasted and then ground. It is said to possess cooling properties and is especially consumed when it is extremely hot.

Kanji — Made from black carrots that sprout very briefly in the season, the carrots are peeled, dried, cut lengthwise, and put in an earthenware pot along with mustard seeds, salt and boiled water. The pot is then kept out in the sun to ferment for five to seven days. The fermented drink is then ready for consumption, and is considered to be very cooling. It is especially regarded to be beneficial for the liver and digestive system.

Siraiki Specialties

Gandal ka saag — Various dishes are made from this indigenous green plant using its young branches and leaves, as it sprouts in winter. It is eaten with whole-wheat bread or fenugreek bread (*missi roti*). The latter consists of whole-wheat bread mixed with fenugreek, masalas, chillies and onions.

Multani Sohan Halwa

Desserts

Sohan halwa — While in Sindh *sohan halwa* is an extremely hard *mithai* shaped like a disc, made with cornflour, sugar, *ghee* and milk and garnished with almonds and pistachios; in southern Punjab *sohan halwa* refers to a soft, sticky *mithai* made with *khoya*, flour, sprouted wheat, ghee and sugar. It is known as *habshi halwa* in Sindh.

Sikh Specialties

Although Sikhs are permitted to eat meat — only if it is slaughtered through the *jhatka* (stunning) process—most Sikhs in Pakistan are vegetarian since meat is slaughtered here in the halal manner. Their basic cuisine comprises vegetables and *chapati*. They often eat *paneer tarkari* as it is a good source of protein.

Desserts

Khara prashad —This special sweet prepared as a holy offering is made from wheat flour, sugar, butter and water. It is generally served to visitors at Gurdwaras (Sikh place of worship) and at funerals. It is similar to *aatay ka halwa* made by some Gujaratis.

Gannay ke ras ki kheer — Made with sugarcane juice and rice, this *kheer* is a favourite with Sikhs.

Pakoray — These are served as appetizers on special occasions, especially at weddings.

8

Balochistan

The Baloch were influenced by Central Asians, migrants from Afghanistan, as well as by the Turks who ruled in this region. Hence, their food habits and cuisine too, reveal the influences of these people. The people of Balochistan are into simple, non-spicy food, similar to the cuisine of their forefathers. The stress is more on nutrients than on flavour. Retaining their ancestral traditions, many still eat on *dastarkhwans*—floor seating for meals—rather than at the dining table.

By and large, the people of Balochistan take two meals a day. For breakfast, they normally prefer *braisni roti* made with butter, cheese and sugar, and tea. The poor population takes bread with onions, chutney and *lassi*—sometimes without the latter—as breakfast. In the higher regions of the province, wheat is the staple diet. Its flour is made into loaves baked on a griddle. Large villages have *daash* or *tandoors* for baking bread. Maize, rice and millets grown in the province are also popular, and milk and its preparations are preferred as accompaniments to the main meal. In the plains, the staple food is bread made of whole-wheat or millet with a decided preference for the former. Cooked pulses and vegetables are also commonly eaten while meat is consumed only occasionally.

Among the well-to-do classes though, the use of *kondi* (dehydrated meat) is common, a tradition that has been passed down by their ancestors who loved to travel and hunt and so were required to carry dry meat for sustenance. *Sajji* also became an integral part of Baloch cuisine because of the nomadic nature of the Baloch tribes, which gave rise to its unique yet practical preparation techniques. Kebabs, on the other hand, are a food item popularized by the Turks which also became popular with affluent Balochs.

While the majority of Makranis also take their meals twice a day, their meals largely consist of dates and milk, the former being the staple food of the people. A shepherd sometimes eats dates for weeks together for all meals. Boiled fish is also popular with Makranis—the gravy is sipped with the dates and the fish is eaten at the end of the meal—

Tandoori Naan

although there are certain types of fish that they do not eat. Among the wealthy, the use of rice at breakfast is common, and wheat loaves and meat are substituted for dates. Fish is popular with them in winter, when it is eaten either fried or as a curry with rice.

Although pulses and vegetables are cooked broadly following the same techniques of cooking as in the rest of the country, there are certain dishes that are quintessentially Baloch and have only over time become popular with other communities as well.

Baloch

Breads

Tandoori roti — Afghani and Baloch in origin, whole-wheat *tandoori rotis* garnished with sesame seeds are baked in *tandoors* or *daashs*.

Khameer roti — Heavier, richer and crustier than the normal *tandoori roti*, the dough of the *khameer roti* has to be mixed with some stale dough—generally leftover from the day before—so that it works as a raising agent and makes the bread fluffy. The tandoor is traditionally, also different—it is a special clay oven called *daash* which is built inside a wall. The dough is placed on a metal plate at the end of an eight feet long stoke and baked in the *daash*. In the days of yore there used to be a *daash* in every area. The dough would be prepared at home and then taken to the *daash* to be cooked. Nowadays, they are rarely to be found.

Muchki — A variety of bread also made in a *daash* but with sugar added to the dough, *muchki* is normally consumed at breakfast.

Meethay parathay/meethi roti — Extremely popular in the rainy season, *gur* is added to its dough before it is kneaded, and the rolled-out dough is either fried or cooked on a *tawa* depending on whether a *paratha* or *roti* is to be made.

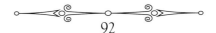

Chawal ki roti — As the name indicates, this bread is made out of rice (*chawal*) flour.

Kaak/kurnu — Popular among the nomadic Balochs, *kaak* is a rock-hard bread, not easily digestible. A blow on the stone breaks open the *kaak*. It is made by wrapping dough round a smooth, blazing hot stone and putting it on embers inside the ground. Most people eat their bread plain and without relish, but *krut* (yogurt pressed in cloth and dried) is sometimes poured over the pieces of bread, to which boiling *ghee* is added. It is also often eaten with *sajji*. Flock owners and camel breeders use milk and its preparations, generally buttermilk, as accompaniments with *kaak*.

Baloch Specialties

Khurood — Essentially a summer dish because of its cooling effect, it is made in the same way as cottage cheese—by putting milk in a muslin cloth and letting the water content drain out. When the milk ferments, it is cooked with salt and made into balls, which are left to dry and harden, in much the same way as the *quroot* made in Afghanistan. In order to be able to eat them, the balls have to be ground—traditionally they were ground over wood, with water sprinkled on the board, though nowadays, blenders are also used for the process—and mixed with water, acquire a soup-like consistency. It is often consumed with pieces of bread soaked in the soup. Variations are now made with chicken pieces added in the balls.

Shorba — The most common and popular Baloch dish is *shorba* (soup) made of meat or of *khurood*. It is similar to *shorwa* made in Afghanistan and thinner in consistency than *aloo gosht* made in Sindh and the Punjab.

Ogra — *Ogra* is porridge made of crushed wheat, millet or maize, rice, white lentils or other food grains, boiled in water with addition of buttermilk or ghee. Sometimes it is made of crushed wild almond fruit (*zarga*). *Ogra* is particularly popular among the Kakar tribe of Balochistan.

Sajji — An Arab delicacy which also became a specialty of Baloch hill tribes, *sajji* or whole roasted lamb is traditionally cooked on a spit of wood struck into the ground and baked over burning wood. Marinated only in salt, it is skewered in a specific way—first the front legs, then the hind legs, followed by the back, ribs and neck. The liver, fats and other parts are not struck into the ground but suspended from a skewer. Retaining its natural moisture and fats, the meat is fully cooked when it turns a golden-brown. It initially became popular with the nomadic Baloch who depended on hunting for their meals, and had no access to stoves or elaborate cooking utensils to prepare their food. Its preparation not only provided much-needed nutrition, it also offered opportunity for camaraderie in a nomadic lifestyle. A convenient, hassle-free meal, *sajji* is traditionally served with *kaak*.

Today, the tradition of cooking and eating *sajji* is closely interwoven in the fabric of Baloch hospitality. Interestingly, there are certain dining etiquettes attached to *sajji* which are inviolable and scrupulously observed. For instance, the back of the animal is left entirely for the hosts to eat. If a woman from the guests' family is married into the host's family, then half the rib-cage is set aside for her. A portion from which meat is never bitten off is the scapula because it is used to foretell the future. The two scapulas complement each other and are never handed over but thrown to the person that wants to read them.

Since the Balochi *sajji* is quite bland in taste, other provinces have come up with spicier variations. In Lahore and Karachi *sajji* is made with whole cooked chicken, incorporating a lot of spices.

Chicken Sajji

Qadeet/Landi — This is basically mutton with its fat dried in the sun with salt. It came into vogue because of the nomadic nature of the tribes which required meat to be preserved for consumption during travel, particularly in the winter months. Providing warmth and nutrition, *qadeet* was and still is the perfect anathema to the severe winters of Balochistan. It is normally eaten with turnips.

Banjan burani — This is an Afghan origin dish that has been adopted by the Baloch. A vegetarian dish, it is made from fried slices of eggplant. The original *burani* made by Afghans incorporates *khurood*, while the Baloch version uses yogurt.

Tireet — Another Arab specialty that has been adopted by Baloch, *tireet* is a clear broth that is a cross between stock and curry. It is eaten with bits of *chapati* broken and soaked into the broth.

Karri — *Karri* is made by drying *lassi* and storing the dried pieces for a few days. Its basic ingredients are yogurt and spices.

Beverages

Zafran sherbet (**saffron drink**) — Introduced by the Mughal Emperor Babar, this Persian drink is served particularly at engagements. It is made with saffron, ground cardamoms, sugar syrup, lime and rose water.

Green tea — Green tea has been consumed in China as a healthful, medicinal drink for the last five thousand years. Not surprisingly it became popular with the communities settled in the northern parts of Pakistan as indeed in other neighbouring areas including Tajikistan, so much so, that with the Pashtuns of Balochistan it became the most frequently consumed drink, taken almost on a daily basis with meals. Balochs now believe they are the only people who know how to make authentic green tea. Water is cooked with green cardamoms and cinnamon prior to adding the tea leaves, and allowed to brew. The beverage is traditionally served in small goblets without handles meant exclusively for serving green tea.

Sewayian (Vermicelli Dessert)

Desserts

Maltashta — A special dish prepared at weddings, it is made with small pieces of bread mixed with sugar and butter.

Shurdee — *Shurdee* is sweet bread, usually pancake-shaped, which is served at the birth of a child in a colourful ceremony called *chatti*.

Zarda — This Mughal dish is made with rice cooked in sweetened water, and orange food colour, topped with dry fruits.

Sewayian — Made with vermicelli fried golden-brown in cardamom-infused ghee and sugar syrup, and garnished with almonds, raisins and pistachios, this dessert is most widely prepared at Eid-ul-Fitr in Balochistan, more so than the *sheerkhurma* that is widely consumed at Eid in the Punjab and Sindh.

Brahuis

Closely linked to the Baloch with whom they have substantially intermingled and whose cultural traits they have absorbed, Brahuis are a Dravidian ethnic group believed to be a remnant of the inhabitants of the Indus Valley Civilization. A variation of 'Barohis' meaning 'mountain dwellers' or 'highlanders', Brahuis live mostly in the rugged hills around the town of Kalat in Balochistan. They cultivate wheat and millet, which are ground into flour and baked into unleavened breads. Rice is also eaten, but usually only on special occasions. Mutton on the other hand, is an important part of the diet of the Brahuis. Food is often eaten from a communal platter. Dates, wild fruits and vegetables are also part of the Brahui diet. Tea is drunk at meals and is also taken as part of various social ceremonies.

Hazaras

Hazaras are a Persian-speaking people residing mainly in Quetta. Genetically, the Hazara are primarily a mixture of eastern Eurasian and western Eurasian peoples. In fact, genetic research suggests that they are closely related to the Mongols and the Uygurs. Their cuisine is similar to that of Afghan immigrants.

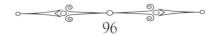

Hazara Specialties

Mantu — Meat dumplings of Uzbek origin, these are filled with onion and ground beef. *Mantu* is steamed and usually topped with a tomato-based sauce and a yogurt-based sauce, and garnished with dried mint.

Delda — This dish is made with split wheat and assorted beans.

Aash — Made with seven main ingredients all boiled separately—strips of thick noodles that are later dried with salt, mince meat, chickpeas, spinach, garlic, *kurut* and Bengal gram—these are all mixed together and then given a *tarka* of *desi ghee*.

Bajindak — A green vegetable similar to spinach, *bajindak* ripens in spring when it is cooked with garlic and eaten as a health sustaining food.

Bosrak — A typically Hazara item, this is a sweet *roti*.

Beverages

Qehwa — Hazaras, like the Kashmiris consume *qehwa* in large quantities—in fact, they drink it like people normally drink water!

Special-Occasion Dishes

Ramazan — A Hazara Iftar favourite is a deep-fried snack of spinach which has been lightly fried with only salt.

Weddings and Funerals

Halwa-e-Samanak — Especially made on the third day after a funeral, or at weddings, this dessert is made with whole wheat flour, yeast and clarified butter. It is cooked for 12 hours till it acquires a thick consistency and a rich colour. Generally made in huge quantities, it is prepared by men of the family as it requires a lot of effort to constantly pummel the ingredients.

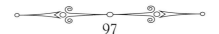

9

Sindh

During the eighth, ninth and tenth centuries AD, Sindhi cooks were famed in the courts of the Caliphs of Baghdad and were sought after in Syria and Iran too. Even today, the variety of dishes prepared from one fish, *palla*, alone is indicative of the richness of variety in Sindhi cuisine. However, while it would not be unusual for meals in an affluent Sindhi household to be exotic, it does not mean that the average indigenous Sindhi family boasts such fare.

Villagers in Sindh ordinarily eat two substantial meals in the day—one some time before noon and the other at eight or nine at night. The normal meal of a peasant in Sindh consists of one or two onions, two thick *chapatis* accompanied with butter, and a glass of buttermilk. In season, certain vegetables are grown and eaten that are not found anywhere else in Pakistan such as *palli* and *chibar*.

Where *jowar* and *bajra* are produced (largely in the desert areas) (Davendra; Thomas; Jabbar and Zerbini 2000) the staple food is *jowar* or *bajri roti*, with *jowar roti* or *paratha* normally consumed in the day. Thanks to limited food resources, roasted locusts are also popular in the Tharparkar region of Sindh. In the mango season the seeds of mangoes are also fried and eaten. People living around the oases in Thar eat eels and catfish cooked as a curry. Wheat bread (*chapati*) is popular with those who can afford it. A sort of porridge made of rice and *daal moong* seasoned with a little salt and *ghee* is often eaten at night.

In rice producing areas, people are used to taking rice at night, along with a fried item like okra or potatoes and a glass of milk, while bread (*chalro*) prepared from rice flour is consumed in the day. In upper Sindh, when weather changes in winter, rice is eaten at lunch and *roti* at night. Sindh is known for producing red rice, which is normally used to make *chapatis*.

Grilled Jumbo Prawns

Grilled whole Pomfret

In coastal areas or near lakes and rivers, fish is consumed practically every day, so much so that what would otherwise be considered a delicacy—lobster biryani—is consumed by the fishermen as a matter of routine. Prawns are often cooked with onions while *palla*, the famous fish of Sindh, considered to have the finest flavour in the east in spite of its multitude of minute bones, is very popular. In season it is eaten for all three meals of the day, either barbecued or fried, in accompaniment with *chapati*, although, many also cook it in curry and eat it with rice. Vegetables and lentils are rarely eaten.

Depending on affordability, the rest of Sindh has staples with vegetables—particularly *saag* in winter—pulses, meat, chicken or fish. The poor at times only eat a meal of dry dates and *gur* with bread in place of vegetables. *Chubars* (fruits), particularly watermelon, milk, buttermilk, and yogurt are generally regarded popular accompaniments.

Other than *pulao, zarda* (also known as *chashney*), *seekh kebabs* and *firni* is also regarded as part of special occasion cuisine in Sindh, as indeed practically all over the country.

Sindhis

Breads

Chanwaran jo atto — Authentic Sindhi bread, it is made out of red rice. This bread has a unique purplish-brown colour and its preparation requires certain amount of expertise so that the texture, thickness and crispness are perfect.

Dho do — Thick *rotis* prepared with masala and garlic paste, they are served with mint chutney.

Rahu paratha — Layers of hand rolled dough that is fried into a *paratha*, it is encrusted with sweet water fish *rahu*.

Bossari or Busri — A rich *roti* prepared with *gur* and *ghee* this bread is normally a breakfast item, especially popular in winter. Similar to the *gogi ki roti* prepared in Khyber Pakhtunkhwa when a girl visits her parent's home the first time after her marriage, this is special bread prepared by the bride's family the day after the wedding.

Sindhi Specialties

Bunda palla machli — Fried, steamed or baked in sand, this fish is delectable in spite of its numerous small bones. After cleaning it and stuffing it with a paste prepared from a variety of spices and herbs, it is cooked on low heat. When baking it in sand, the *palla* is wrapped in cloth, and buried three feet deep in hot sand under the sun. It bakes, thus, for four to five hours, from late morning to early afternoon.

There are two folklores surrounding *palla* in Sindh. One attributes its popularity to King Jamtamachee. According to the folklore the king was smitten by Noori, the daughter of a Sindhi fisherman. So enamoured was he with her that he was willing to give up his empire for her hand in marriage, while the entire fishing community was up in arms about the proposal. In order to try and woo the community, the king gifted the people lots of land,

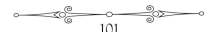

and whenever he visited them he would be served *palla machli*, which became a special delicacy to serve to visitors.

According to another tale, when Muhammed Tughlaq invaded Sindh, he was offered *palla* fish. He liked it so much that he consumed huge quantities of it, which caused his death. That's why *palla* fish came to be known as 'Enemy Defeater'.

Machli ke kebab — Fillet of fish marinated in rich spices and shaped into *kebabs*, they are skewered and char-grilled in the *tandoor*.

Pulao — Basically made the same way as in other parts of the country, and indeed in neighbouring countries, the difference in the Sindhi *pulao* and other *pulaos* made by Tajiks or Pashtuns lies in the ingredients used. Unlike in the other two *pulaos* dry fruits and vegetables such as carrots or turnips are not incorporated, and the dish normally comprises rice, potatoes and one meat item, be it chicken, mutton, prawn or fish.

Sindhi Kukar — Spicy blackened chicken, this dish has a smoky flavour, achieved by adopting the *dhuan* technique of cooking.

Acho Bor — White curry made with lightly fried chicken mixed with yogurt, ground onions, almonds and *sabut garam masala*, it doesn't go through the *bhoonna* process, and is put on *dum* till cooked. It is generally a must in big family gatherings.

Bhindhi basar — Spiced okra, this vegetarian dish is prepared with julienne onions and tomatoes.

Tali hui bhindi — Chopped fine and fried crisp, this is a delicious dish made with okra that has been washed and dried in the sun and then stir-fried with salt and red chillies.

Daal — Different from the *daals* made by other communities, this liquid *daal* does not have the usual *tarka*, and is sprinkled with tangy masala.

Teetar — Basically a winter speciality, this delicacy is prepared by turning partridges (*teetar*) on a spit over a campfire. When prepared inside homes, *teetar* is normally fried.

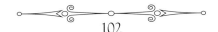

Langar — A simple dish made at deaths, it is prepared with *chanay ki daal*, rice and *gur*. In fact, the name *langar* means communal feast.

Karelay — A particularly popular vegetable, *karelay* (bitter gourd) is prepared in a variety of ways in Sindh. It is fried on its own with masala, and is also enjoyed cooked with *chanay ki daal* or with mutton.

Machli kofta — This dish comprises fish balls gently poached in an aromatic curry.

Mangro qeema — A unique dish made of shark mince, it is cooked with spices.

Murgh sajji — Unlike the Baloch *sajji* made of lamb, this version is made with spiced whole chicken slow roasted over a wood fire.

Anar gosht fry — Sautéed cubes of meat, this delicious dish is gently coated with pummelled pomegranate.

Beh — Lotus root, generally baked in a clay *handhi*, it can be prepared in many different ways, such as by frying, or stuffing with mince.

Desserts

Halwas — These have been brought by the Arabs to Sindh. Although there are many variations, it generally takes the form of a sesame paste sweet, usually made in a slab, and studded with fruits and nuts. Another popular halwa variety is softer and wetter, made basically out of a seasonal fruit or vegetable—although gram flours and wheat flour are just as common—and ubiquitously served as dessert when the fruit or vegetable is in full season. Popular variations include *suji ka halwa* (made with semolina), *anday ka halwa* (made with eggs), *aata ka halwa* (made with wheat flour), *lawki ka halwa* (made with pumpkin), *gajar ka halwa* (made with carrots), *chanay ka halwa* (made with golden yellow lentils) and *khajoor ka halwa* (made with dates).

Penhon — Dessert made of crushed rice and cooked in sugar water, it is served normally at breakfast, especially the day after a wedding.

Tahiri — *Gur* or raw sugar rice cooked with dry fruits, this dish is generally cooked on special occasions such as when celebrating the birth of a boy, or during the rainy season.

Beverages

Thadal — A refreshing drink normally prepared in summer, it is made from the extract of dried fruit seeds such as watermelon and almonds, and aromatics.

Abresham — This is a herb-extract drink sweetened to taste.

Imli aur aloo bukharay ka sherbet — Made of tamarind and dried apricots, this is a refreshing drink served in summer months.

Gannay ka ras — With sugarcane in abundance, this pure sugarcane juice is a popular drink all over the Sindh province. In the Punjab, it is seasoned with ginger and lime.

Accompaniments

Shikarpur ka achar — This *achar* may be sweet or sour, and based in oil or water.

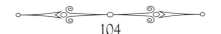

Aloo ka Bhurta

Hindus

Although Hindus in Pakistan are spread out throughout the country, they are concentrated in the rural areas of Sindh, while a substantial number also live in the cities, such as in Karachi. By and large Hindus do not eat beef as they regard cows as sacred; many are semi-vegetarian, avoiding red meat altogether, and only occasionally allowing themselves to eat fish or chicken. However, interestingly enough, Hindus living in the larger cities of Pakistan have adapted themselves to Pakistani culture to such a great extent that many have begun to even eat beef, what to talk of mutton and other meats.

Nonetheless, their style of cooking remains distinct, and although many of their specialties are made by other communities as well, such as by Muslim Gujaratis, some of the ingredients used in Hindu cuisine, like *heeng* (asafoetida) are peculiar only to their foods, and rarely used by the other Pakistani communities. Similarly, most Hindu dishes are prepared in green chutney—made with ground mint and coriander leaves—and the use of *garam masala* otherwise common in Pakistani cuisine is minimal. Another peculiarity of Hindu cuisine is that meat items are cooked separately from vegetarian ones and the two are rarely, if ever, combined.

Among the poorer Hindus, *lapsi karhi, palak paneer* and soybean are popular dishes. However, in the desert regions of Sindh, Hindu inhabitants have a distinct cuisine. Though the emphasis is more on nutrition than on fuss and ostentation, given the harsh climatic conditions, it is commendable that the Hindus of Thar have produced so much variety from so little. They are strict vegetarians and will not even use garlic and onion in their cuisine. Dried lentils and beans from indigenous plants are the staples of their diet. Millet and maize are used for making various kinds of bread. They use a lot of pulses and gram flour in their cuisine as vegetables are scarce in the desert climate. *Moong daal ki khilni* (a dry preparation of lentils, tossed in a mixture of spices), *moong godi ki subzi* (grape-size dumplings of green gram, which have been ground to a paste and sun-dried), and *gatte ki subzi* (rolls of gram flour, steamed and cooked in buttermilk sauce) are delicacies in this region. Other innovations include the use of mango powder as a substitute for tomatoes, and asafoetida to enhance taste in the absence of garlic and onions. Sweets are also very popular.

Breads

Sail phulka — Small, fluffy *chapatis* these *phulkas* are dipped in green chutney and then steam-cooked.

Hindu Specialties

Dhoklay — A Gujarati specialty, the snack is as popular with Muslim Gujaratis as with Hindus. These are spongy, savoury, steamed cakes made from fermented chickpea or gram flour or rice and eaten with spicy red chutney.

Besan ki bhaji — This vegetarian dish is made by *bhoonoing* gram flour in masalas and onions and then making *tikyas* (flat balls) out of it and cooking them in onion-based gravy.

Idli — Steamed rice cakes, *idlis* are a south Indian specialty that became very popular with Gujaratis—both Hindu and Muslim—who were largely vegetarian at one point.

Dhokri — These are millet dumplings (*dhokri*) that are cooked in green chutney curry and then vegetables such as potatoes, okra, chillies and onions are added to it. The *dhokris* are steamed in the gravy so that they imbibe all the flavours of the different ingredients.

Masala dosa — The *dosa* is traditionally made of a thin crispy crepe stuffed with spicy potatoes and served with coconut chutney and *sambhar* made of lentils. According to a legend, *masala dosa* was introduced when the king of Mysore hosted a big festival and ordered his cook to reuse the leftovers to avoid wastage. The chef came up with the brilliant idea of stuffing a plain dosa with potatoes and spices, thus the arrival on the culinary scene of this delectable dish. Since Pakistanis are basically meat eaters, local variations of this delicacy, such as chicken *dossa* have come into existence and have become highly popular.

Desserts

Gehar — Mainly eaten on the Hindu Holi festival, this sweet item is similar to a large *jalebi*.

Lai — A paper-thin *chikee* (a brittle, caramelized sweet made with peanuts, mixed nuts or sesame seeds), it is normally made on Diwali, another Hindu festival, especially by Sindhi Hindus.

Masala Dosa

10

Karachi Cuisine

Karachiites, rich and poor alike, love to eat, and generally are more willing to experiment with their cuisine than those living in any other part of the country. This cosmopolitan city is home to not only people who have settled here from other regions of the country, but also to a variety of different ethnic communities. Although within a given socio-economic set up their basic meals may not have varied greatly, their specialties cooked on important occasions were once worlds apart. Today though, with the growing trend for assimilating cultures, one may eat a dish peculiar to one community in other communities as well. They are no longer as great a novelty to the rest of the Karachiites as they used to be.

Generally, breakfast in Karachi does not vary so much owing to people's ethnicity as owing to their income. In the middle and upper classes, bread is normally eaten with eggs, jam or cheese. Cereals often form popular substitutes or accompaniments. Tea is an almost universal favourite, although among the more affluent classes coffee is also favoured. Over the weekends, or on public holidays, a more lavish breakfast is normally partaken, comprising *aloo ki bhujia*, *cholay*, *halwa* and *puris*. Breakfast for the lower income groups normally comprises *chapatis* and leftover curry from the night before.

Meat consumption is heavy in the city, while prawns, shrimps, and a variety of fish including pomfret, elicia and carp are often used as substitutes for meat. The staple food at lunch and dinner in upper income groups is a meat curry with *chapati*, and some vegetable or lentil dish on the side. But usually meals depend on the affordability of a household, and the main dish is accordingly, either a meat or vegetable or lentils dish. Many households also serve boiled rice as staple for at least one meal.

Among desserts, *shahi tukray* are a specialty while in winter *gajar ka halwa* is a popular delicacy.

While typically, curry, and *chapati* or rice form the staple food of Karachiites, the multi-ethnic composition of the city, as stated earlier, has given rise to the adoption of a vast variety of cuisine that was once popular only in the communities from which they originated. The upper strata of society, which can afford to regularly eat out or cook cuisine that involve imported ingredients or different cooking styles, has begun to frequently partake of dishes that were once alien to them. An example of a foreign cuisine that has become almost universally popular among Karachiites in particular, is Chinese. In fact, so localized have the Cantonese and Schezwan styles patronized in Karachi become, that Chinese food has taken on a completely new dimension here.

Along with the Chinese community that settled in Karachi after Partition, although, some were there from before Partition—many of whom opened restaurants and were responsible for introducing their cuisine to the country—several other communities including the Urdu-speaking, commonly referred to as Muhajirs (migrants), Anglo-Indians, Goans, Khojas, Gujaratis, Bohras, Memons, Hindus, and Parsis also made this city their home, and not only brought their specialties along with them, but were also successful in popularizing them outside their communities.

The Anglo-Indians, for instance, are a community whose impact on the cuisine has been felt not just in Karachi, the first city in Pakistan to receive their influence, but in the smaller towns and villages as well. The ubiquitous plain cake, so popular with tea even at *chai ka addas*, is one example of a food item that owes its popularity to the synthesizing capability of this community.

The Urdu-speaking or Mohajir community hail from different parts of India and as such their cuisine varies, depending on their roots. In Karachi, the Urdu-speaking communities that have come to be known for their cuisine hail from Lucknow, Hyderabad Deccan, Delhi and Bihar. Each possesses their own set of specialties, and over the years Karachiites in general have acquired a taste for them.

Other types of cuisine that have become popular in Karachi and other major cities of Pakistan owe their popularity not so much to the communities that have settled here and introduced them as to the increasing trend for embracing different cuisines and opening niche restaurants. Hence, we have Italian pizzas and pastas; American burgers and steaks; Arab shawarmas; Japanese sushis and tempuras and a lot more offered in a large number of restaurants and even cooked in many homes, today. The proliferation of cooking shows on television channels has also been responsible for the widespread popularity of, and familiarity with, international cuisines.

Dilliwallay

The Mughal era is unrivalled in its display of hospitality and its attention to style and luxury. Its cuisine is one of the many legacies bequeathed to the subcontinent by its rulers, perhaps more evident in Delhi than in any other city. Many of the specialties of Dilliwallay brought with them to Pakistan, not surprisingly, are of Mughal origin. These include:

Breads

Baqerkhani — Unlike the Kashmiri *baqerkhani* this one is made of flour kneaded with milk, *ghee* and sugar, and cooked in a *tandoor*. *Ghee* is then applied on the *roti* and holes pierced on it. It is normally eaten with *aloo gosht*.

Taftan — A leavened rice flour bread originating from Persian cuisine, it incorporates sugar, milk and lemon seeds, and is baked in a clay oven. *Taftans* are popular at weddings. They are normally eaten with *shab daigh*.

Daal bharay parathay — Flat bread made with whole-wheat flour and stuffed with boiled, ground *chanay ki daal* mixed with roasted cumin, red chillies and salt, it is then deep fried.

Raway ke parathay — Made of *suji* and eaten with sweet and savoury dishes, this bread is also cooked in a *tandoor* and is particularly popular on Eid. It is often eaten with mangoes during the mango season.

Nihari

Dilliwallay Specialties

Nihari — Perhaps, the most popular dish in Pakistan today originating from Delhi is *nihari*, generally believed to have been originally cooked by a hakim (one who prescribes treatment through herbs). While once it was served only as a breakfast item in winters in the upscale households of Delhi, hence the name—*nihar* means first thing in the morning—it has over the years become a much sought-after dinner delicacy by all income groups.

According to one legend, Emperor Shah Jehan asked his cooks to conjure a dish that would be able to sustain the labourers during the day while they worked on the construction of the Taj Mahal, and they came up with *nihari*. According to yet another legend, during the reign of Shah Jehan, Delhi's water supply, which came from a canal in the middle of Chandini Chowk, for some reason became suspect. The hakims, as a remedy came up with a recipe for this beef stew with lots of red chillies that were supposed to have germ killing properties. Regardless of whether this remedy was successful or not, there is no denying that it became very popular.

Nihari is prepared by cooking large pieces of beef shank, along with bones and spices, over low heat, generally overnight. The bones are later taken out and discarded and the curry is thickened by adding wheat flour to it. The longer the curry is allowed to cook, the more delectable the *nihari* tastes.

Shola — Different from the *shola* made in Khyber Pakhtunkhwa, this dish is basically a local version of shepherd's pie. It is made with rice and lentils cooked with leftover food such as *qeema*, *saag*, and chillies.

Baryan — Small *urad ki daal* or *moong ki daal ke pakoray*, the *daal* is soaked overnight and coarsely ground, then mixed with spices and aromatics and kept out to dry. The dumplings are lightly fried and immersed in curry.

Khandvian — A paste made with *besan* and spices and allowed to set, it is cut into squares after it becomes hard, and cooked in curry made with spices and yogurt.

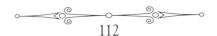

Kalmi baray — *Daal bhajias*, these are fried dumplings cut in wedges and then re-fried.

Saim ke beej ka salan — This seasonal dish comprises seeds of *saim ki phalli* (broad beans) cooked in regular *gosht ka salan*. It is cooked only in winter when the *saim ki phalli* are in season.

Long cheray — These are basically *besan kebabs* which, like *seekh kebabs*, are grilled on skewers. They are particularly popular in Ramazan.

Shab daigh — This is a beautiful blend of whole or halved carrots—as opposed to turnips that are a part of the same dish prepared in Kashmir—tender mutton pieces or minced mutton shaped into meatballs and cooked over low heat all night (hence the *shab* in the name, meaning 'night'), in *daighs*, sealed with dough, the result is an incredibly rich and flavourful gravy with gentle spices, saffron and seasoning. These days, many people have begun to incorporate both turnips and carrots in the dish. The culinary skill of a cook in preparing this dish lies in the deftness with which all the meatballs and carrots are made to look like one another and cooked to perfection of texture. It is usually garnished with fresh green chillies and coriander.

Maash ki daal — Basically white lentil, *mash ki daal* is boiled with salt, and at the most, green chillies and ginger. It is then given a *tarka* of fried onions and garnished with mint, coriander and lime.

Dhaga kebab — Also known as *gola kebab*, this tenderized minced meat kebab dish derives its name from the thread used to wrap up the kebabs on skewers before they are barbecued.

Qeema bharay karelay — A dish to set before a king! Bitter gourd filled with *qeema* and *chanay ki daal* and cooked on *dum* for three to four hours, it is a tricky dish to make as the bitterness has to be removed from the gourd in the cooking process.

Aloo salan — Known as *aloo gosht* or *gosht ka salan* in other communities, this is a mutton and potato curry cooked in basic spices. It is perhaps, the most widely consumed curry dish in the country.

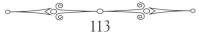

Stew — Onion plays a main role in this traditionally mutton dish which also incorporates whole spices and yogurt.

Gosht khara masala — Similar to stew, this dish incorporates tomatoes instead of yogurt.

Katchnar — This is a *bhujia* (vegetables in gravy) made in winter with buds that begin to appear on the *katchnar* plant (deciduous trees of the Bauhinieae plant family).

Imli ke phool — This dish consists of tamarind flowers cooked with mutton *qeema* and onions.

Peethi ki kachori — This is a fried, layered *puri* stuffed with masala or a variety of fillings which include mince, vegetables, or *daals*, especially *urad ki daal*. It is eaten normally on special occasions or in Ramazan and on Eid.

Desserts

Kulfi/kulfa — Rich and creamy, made with condensed/evaporated milk, saffron, almonds and cashew nuts, this frozen milk dessert has come to be regarded as a *desi* version of

Kulfi

un-churned ice-cream and is normally served with *falooda*. The latter are arrowroot noodles that are boiled and then simmered in milk and cooled over ice.

Originating in Persia, *kulfi* is believed to have been introduced in the subcontinent to please the palate of the great Mughal Emperor Akbar, and developed further by later Mughals. The Mughals brought ice to Delhi from a mountain near Kasauli called *Choori Chandni ka Dhar* which is perennially covered with snow. The method of making *kulfi* has remained unchanged to the present day. Thickened milk is put into special conical moulds and frozen by putting the moulds in a large pot filled with a mixture of ice and salt, which is shaken gently till the *kulfi* freezes. The moulds can be of metal, but the traditional earthenware moulds give the *kulfi* a lovely flavouring.

Gajar batta — This dessert is basically *gaajar ka halwa* cooked in water but served with milk and cream.

Rabri — This calorie-laden sweet dish is made by evaporating milk over low heat till it becomes dense and changes colour. Although the addition of fresh cream, butter and sugar gives the *rabri* a curdled-milk texture, it tastes divine.

Kheer — Made with rice, milk and sugar, this sweet dish is extremely popular throughout the country.

Qalaqand — Made from solidified, sweetened milk and cottage cheese, this sweet is garnished with pistachios.

Hyderabadis

The history of Hyderabadi cuisine begins in the seventeenth century, with the Deccan campaigns. Over a period of nearly a century, the Mughal armies annexed great areas of southern India to their territories. Over the years, the Mughlai cuisine brought from the north slowly evolved influenced by the local ingredients, climate and cuisines encountered along the way. A blend of the Mughlai flavours passed down from the renowned chefs of the royal families or Nizams of Hyderabad and the cuisine of its Hindu majority population,

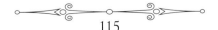

Haleem

which commonly employed coconut, tamarind, jaggery and mustard seeds, gave rise to a distinct rich style of food preparation. In fact, its singular and most distinguishing feature was the sourness or tanginess of its dishes. Hyderabadi Muslims brought with them the richness of their cuisine when they moved to Pakistan and succeeded in popularising it so much that today many of their specialties are cooked by other ethnic groups in Karachi as well. Among the most popular Hyderabadi dishes are:

Bagharay baingan — This is a festive dish in which small and tender eggplants are partially quartered and stuffed with a spicy, sour, sweet and salty mixture (a combination including coconut, tamarind, jaggery and mustard seeds) and cooked on low heat. A final *baghar* or pouring of hot oil flavoured with spices gives the finishing touch to the dish.

Haleem — *Haleem* is originally a Persian dish. It is a thick, pasty, high calorie dish which became popular with the Mughal emperors and, subsequently, became a renowned delicacy at the hands of Hyderabad's chefs. Although the dish varies in form from region to region, it generally includes cracked grains of wheat, two kinds of pulses—*chana* and *moong*—spices and meat (usually beef or mutton, but sometimes chicken or minced meat). This dish is cooked for seven to eight hours, all the while being vigorously stirred so that the lentils and wheat are crushed into a smooth paste, before it is ready to be served. Since it is packed with nutrients, it is an instant energy giver, and is particularly popular at meals after breaking a fast. It is associated with the tenth of Muharram, a day of mourning and usually a day of fasting. *Haleem* is garnished with crispy fried onions, chopped green chillies, julienne ginger and a touch of lemon. Sister versions of the dish are known as *khichra* and *harisa*.

Hyderabadi biryani — Also known as *kachay gosht ki biryani* (raw meat *biryani*) as unlike the other *biryanis* it is prepared with marinated, raw meat that is cooked only through the process of *dum*, Hyderabadi *biryani* is a combination of the two different kinds of *biryanis*

Til ki Chutney

that were introduced into the subcontinent—one by the Persians which is a mild version; and the other by the Mughals which incorporates a lot of spices. The Hyderabadi version is neither too spicy, nor too mild.

Dum ke kebab — Made with undercut that has been marinated with salt and raw papaya, *dum ke kebabs* are cooked on low heat basically with yogurt and a paste of poppy seeds, almonds, cumin and coconut.

Chaakna — This is a spicy stew made out of goat tripe, intestines and other digestive parts, cooked with flour.

Qeema sewaiyan — An interesting combination of ingredients, this dish consists of minced meat (mutton) cooked in masalas, fried onions, tomatoes and yogurt. Roasted vermicelli and lemon juice is added to the cooked mince before it is put on *dum*.

Hari mirch aur qeema — Made with minced beef, this dish comprises mince marinated in yogurt and spices and cooked with onions and lots of water. The green chillies (*hari mirch*) are added halfway through the cooking and the dish is allowed to simmer until the water dries up.

Khatti daal — Different kinds of *khatti* (tangy) *daal* are commonly made by Hyderabadis. These could be *kairi ki daal* (with raw mango), *kacchi imli ki daal* (raw green tamarind *daal*), *nimboo daal* (with lemon juice) or the regular *khatti daal* comprising yellow lentils made with blended tamarind pulp, tomatoes and spices.

Acharee murghi — Made in mustard oil with ground roasted spices, whole spices, onions and tomatoes this chicken dish has a tangy taste.

Til ki chutney — Made with green chillies, fresh coriander and garlic pummelled together and combined with ground, roasted sesame seeds and tamarind juice, this is mouth-watering chutney. It is eaten especially with *matar pulao*.

Adus pulao — Basically a Persian style of cooking rice with lentils, raisins and dates, this dish is very nutritious.

Sheerkhurma

Mirch ka salan — Comprising whole green chillies pan-fried and simmered in sesame-peanut spicy sauce, this is a nutritious dish that has a tantalizing taste.

Tomato kutt — This Hyderabadi specialty is eaten as a side dish, usually as an accompaniment to *pulao* or fried rice. Made with blanched and pureed tomatoes cooked with roasted and ground onions and roasted and pummelled spices, this vegetarian dish is a great favourite with food lovers.

Tas kebab — Of Turkish origin, this meat dish is commonly eaten with vegetable *pulao*. Vegetables are first cooked in butter and then beef is stewed in it. The layers of beef are spiced up with onions and masala.

Lukmiya — Square samosay (fried wafer shells) made with flour, water, milk and oil. These days they also have a filling of cottage cheese, although the original version was made only with minced mutton.

Daalcha — Made with mutton and *chanay ki daal* this is another popular lentil dish.

Desserts

Khobani ka meetha — A favourite with Hyderabadis *Khobani ka meetha* or apricot custard is made in a variety of ways. Generally, it is made with dried apricots that have been boiled and mashed and then served with custard and fresh cream.

Double ka meetha — Fried double *rotis* (slices of a loaf of bread)—thus its name—cooked with milk, sugar, saffron and *khoya*, this dessert is similar to *shahi tukray* and is served on special occasions such as weddings.

Puran puri — These are semolina and flour pastries that are filled with sugar, dry fruits and coconut, and deep fried.

Sheerkhurma — Made with milk, vermicelli, sugar and *mewa*, this dessert is especially associated with Eid.

Malida — This rich dessert is made by frying whole-wheat *puris* that are pounded and cooked in sweetened milk and garnished with almonds.

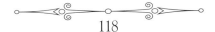

Bihari Kebab

Biharis

The Biharis are an ethnic group originating from the state of Bihar in India with a history going back to three millennia. Their ancestry can be traced to the Munda inhabitants of the region as well as to the Indo-Aryans.

At the time of Partition many Muslim Biharis migrated to East Bengal (East Pakistan and subsequently Bangladesh), while a substantial number settled in Karachi (in West Pakistan). The formation of Bangladesh resulted in an increase in the number of Biharis moving to Karachi as refugees fleeing from the former eastern wing of Pakistan, thus increasing Karachiites' exposure to Bihari cuisine.

Breads

Kulchay — Special Bihari *naans*, *kulchas* are bread made with milk, flour, yeast and sugar, sprinkled with sesame seeds, and normally eaten for breakfast with *malai*. They could contain various fillings such as onions, cottage cheese and cauliflower.

Besan ki roti — Made with *besan aata*, red chilli powder, finely chopped onions, salt and turmeric powder these are eaten with *achar*, and chopped onions marinated in mustard oil.

Peetha — Made with rice flour and poppy seeds, this bread is steamed. It is normally eaten with *butt* (see specialties).

Bihari Specialties

Bihari kebab — Succulent and tender variety of charcoal grilled meats, this is perhaps the most popular Bihari dish in the country. This skewer of beef mixed with herbs, seasonings, raw papaya and onions, is unique in that mustard oil is used in its preparation, while traditionally, garlic is not used. Although the origin of the dish can be traced to Bihar, it is

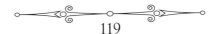

Kalay Chanay

believed that the person responsible for introducing it to Karachi was a man called Jumbo Khan living in Orangi Town. Strangely enough, instead of eating it with *parathay* as is usually the case wherever *Bihari kebab* is prepared in the country, Biharis prefer to eat it with plain boiled rice and *daal*. Alternatively, it is also eaten with *baqerkhani*. Interestingly, it is also often eaten with *puris* or *parathay* made with the left-over marinade of the *Bihari kebab* and wheat flour.

Kachri — *Masoor ki daal ke pakoray*, these are fried fritters that are crispier than their counterparts made of *besan*.

Kalay chanay (also known as ghungri) — Boiled black chickpeas cooked in mustard oil with brown onions, cumin, black pepper and crushed red chillies, the dish is garnished with coriander leaves and eaten as a snack. It is particularly popular in Ramazan for Iftari.

Koftay — Made with the inclusion of soya, these mince meat balls are different in taste from the *koftay* made by other communities.

Aloo ki bhujia — These are potatoes cooked in gravy made with onions, cumin, whole red chillies, and black pepper.

Daal peethi — Little flowers made with whole-wheat flour, these are cooked in *masoor ki daal* and given a *baghar* of whole red chillies and cumin. It is eaten in accompaniment with *achar*.

Khichri — Made with *masoor ki daal* that is over-cooked in lots of water, and has whole mixed spices and whole red chillies. It is always served with four accompaniments—*aloo ka bhurta*, fried onions in mustard oil, tomato chutney and *achar*.

Tahri — Rice with potatoes and green peas, this dish is cooked in tomatoes, masala, green chillies and coriander. It is normally served with *kofta* curry and *tamatar ka bhurta*.

Butt — A delicacy, it comprises intestines and soya and is cooked slowly into a curry.

Jehangiri — This is whole chicken stuffed with an assortment of vegetables and then baked.

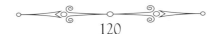

Snacks

Shakarpaala — Made with flour and clarified butter, it is cut into small pieces and deep fried. *Shakarpala* is then dipped in sugar syrup and cooled.

Khormi — Similar to *shakarpaala*, the only difference is that *khormi* is not dipped in sugar syrup.

Kulchi — This snack is made with flour, semolina, a touch of sugar, and salt, kneaded into dough, then cut into shapes brushed with milk and poppy seeds, and baked in an oven.

Saank — Made with flour, clarified butter, salt and onion seeds, the ingredients are kneaded into a dough, rolled out and cut into strips and deep fried.

Chanay ki daal — Soaked overnight, this crunchy *chanay ki daal* dish is particularly popular at Iftari. It is seasoned with lemon juice, salt and black pepper, and garnished with green chillies and onions.

Desserts

Guramba — This dessert is made with mangoes brought to a boil. The blanched mangoes are then mixed with boiled jaggery and water, and cooked together. The strained pulp is given a *baghar* with cloves, cardamoms and flour before it is ready to be served.

Maquti — Similar to *firni*, *maquti* is made with *moong ki daal*, little rice, milk and sugar.

Mangochi — Made with *moong ki dal* and *maash ki daal* soaked and ground separately and then mixed to form a batter that is deep fried, the fritters are then dipped in sugar syrup.

Beverages

Amori/keri ka sherbet — Made with boiled raw mangoes that are blended and cooked with sugar and water, this refreshing drink tastes best when served chilled with a dash of lemon juice and black salt.

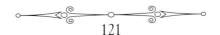

Shami Kebab

Luknawis

Awadhi or Luknawi cuisine has its origin in the city of Lucknow, the capital of the state of Uttar Pradesh located in northern India. The cooking patterns of the people hailing from there are similar to that of people belonging to Central Asia, the Middle East and other parts of northern India. Greatly influenced by Mughal cooking techniques, Luknawi cuisine particularly bears similarities to the cuisines of Kashmir and Hyderabad, and is famous for its 'Nawabi' foods particularly kebabs made with minced meat or meat paste as opposed to skewered kebabs.

While drawing on exotic spices and creams to enrich their dishes, the *bawarchis* (chefs) of Awadh concentrated on the *dum* style of cooking or the art of cooking over very low heat, so much so that it has become synonymous with Luknawi cuisine today. The Luknawis of the eighteenth century particularly prided themselves in having perfected the Mughlai *qorma* (Collingham 2006) and the Central Asian inspired *pulao*.

Breads

Sheermal — Originating in Iran, *sheermal* is believed to have been introduced to Lucknow by a cook named Muhamdoo during the period of Nawab Nasir-ud-din Haider. It is prepared with sweetened warm milk, flour and eggs, thus its name: *sheer* means milk. The bread's soft, smooth texture and appealing look—its crust is full of holes—not to mention its unique taste, makes it a vital part of food served at marriages.

Rumaali roti — The Urdu word *rumaali* literally means 'handkerchief', and *Rumaali roti* is an elaborately and dexterously prepared ultra thin bread made on a huge convex metal pan from finely ground wheat flour. It is a treat to watch one of these being prepared with great flourish by skilled cooks.

Parathay — Luknawi *parathay* are made from whole-wheat flour, and lack the many layers that characterize most *parathay*. *Parathay* stuffed with different fillings such as *chanay ki daal*, *besan* and potatoes are very popular.

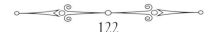

Luknawi Specialties

Dum pukht — A style of cooking that originated in Persia some two hundred years ago and was enjoyed by the Nawabs of Awadh *dum pukht* is a process of cooking using the *dum* technique. A number of different kinds of dishes are made by Luknawis involving this style of cooking, the most popular among them being the emptying out of the insides of a lamb and stuffing it with rice, almonds and raisins and then cooking it slowly in its own steam.

Another dish employing this technique of cooking is made with a layer of cut-up potatoes topped with meat, yogurt, turmeric, fat, and whole red chillies, and cooked overnight on low heat. Variations with pulses, called *namkeen* are also popular.

Galavat kebab — According to one story pertaining to the origin of this aromatic and light kebab, in the early 1900s, a small village near Lucknow called Kakori acquired fame for their melt-in-the-mouth, smoked mince kebabs served to the toothless pilgrims that would visit it, as the shrine of a Sufi saint was located there. The mince for the kebab was reputed to be made from the tendon of leg of lamb. The fat content was replaced by *khoya*, black pepper by white pepper, and a special mix of powdered spices was added to create the perfect blend. The recipe was later taken to Lucknow, where this *galavati kebab* became a specialty, and later immigrants to Pakistan brought the tantalizing recipe with them.

According to another story, the residents of Lucknow, particularly members of the nobility, considered it uncouth to be seen biting into meat or chewing it. The cooks in the court circles were therefore ordered to device delicacies that would avoid mastication. Meats were tenderized by an application of raw papaya paste, and for kebabs, only thrice minced cuts were used. According to this legend the person credited with the creation of this famous tenderized kebab is Tunda, a cook who lived more than a hundred years ago. He was nicknamed Tunda because he had lost an arm in an accident in his adolescence. His recipe, handed down to generations continues to delight the palate with its pate like consistency and wonderful aromatics.

Shami kebab — Introduced to the subcontinent during Babar's time in the Mughal era, (Collingham 2006), *shami kebab* is a small patty of minced beef, mutton or chicken, and

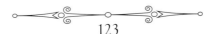

Seekh Kebab

ground chickpeas and spices, originally cooked in earthen pots. According to one legend they were made of soft, fine, lamb mince (ideally like velvet) so that the toothless Nawab Asaf-ud-Daulah could eat this refined version of the Central Asian and Afghani kebab (Collingham 2006).

Traditionally, the preparation of *shami kebabs* required no *bhoonoing*, and the meat used to be tenderized by cooking it in its own steam by sealing the lid of the *degchi* tightly with *aata* paste. Today, it is prepared in many different ways depending on personal and familial tastes and conveniences.

The origin of the name of the dish is a mystery though. One belief is that 'Sham' refers to either Syria specifically, or the Levant in general and these kebabs literally mean Syrian kebabs or Levantine kebabs in Arabic. The other belief is that *sham* (meaning 'evening' in Urdu) refers to *sham-e-Awadh*—evening in Lucknow—as it was a popular evening snack there. A parochial perfumer from Kannauj offered yet another explanation, linking the spices used in it with the seductive whiff of an *itr* (non-alcoholic perfume) called *shamama*.

Seekh kebab — Turkish tradition has it that this dish was invented by medieval Turkic soldiers who used their swords to grill meat over open-field fires. Minced beef mixed with herbs and seasonings, grilled over charcoals on skewers called *seekhs*—hence its name—*seekh kebab* was introduced in this region by Emperor Babar. It became a *piece de resistance* in the Luknawi *dastarkhwan*, originally prepared from beef mince wrapped around iron skewers and cooked on charcoal fire. Later influences and innovations led to the use of lamb mince, which was preferred for its soft texture. Besides, serving of it on the *dastarkhwan* did not offend the sensibilities of the Hindu guests. Gradually, the *seekh kebab* found its way into other communities as well.

Kakori kebab — The immense popularity of the *seekh kebab* led to further refinements and improvements, and one *bawarchi* from Kakori—a small hamlet on the outskirts of Lucknow of *galavat kebab* fame—found much acclaim for his efforts in this direction. During British rule, it was customary in this region for the rich Rajas and Nawabs to entertain senior British officers and ply them with the best hospitality they could offer. At one such party in Kakori, stung by the remark of a British officer regarding the coarse texture of *seekh kebab*, the host, Nawab Syed Mohammad Haider Kazmi summoned his cooks and asked them to evolve a more refined version of the *seekh kebab*. The result was the now famous *Kakori kebab* which was as close to perfection as possible. Of course, the Nawab invited the same officer again and presented him with the new version. Needless to say, it met with great applause. Since then the *seekh kebabs* of Kakori have become famous and have acquired the universal name of *Kakori kebabs*.

Koftay — Of Middle Eastern and Central Asian origin, *koftas* were introduced to the Indian subcontinent through the various invasions; adopted by the Mughals; and perfected by Luknawis. These are balls of minced or ground meat, usually beef or lamb, generally cooked with gravy, though they are occasionally baked or charcoal grilled on skewers.

Nargisi koftay — An exotic curry-based dish, it derives its name from the jasmine flower (known as *nargis*) which is a white flower with a yellow centre, as this dish comprises meatballs with a centre of boiled eggs.

Nargisi Koftay

Baingan ka bhurta — Made with roasted mashed eggplants, this delicious side dish is cooked with spices and onions.

Palak paneer — Originating in Persia, this spinach dish was introduced to the region by the Mughals. This lightly cooked vegetarian platter has chunks of fried cottage cheese in it.

Desserts

Kadoo ka halwa — Made with grated yellow pumpkin, dried milk, sugar and cream, this dessert is a favourite throughout the year as pumpkins are available in all seasons.

Gulgulay — Made with jaggery, sesame seeds, eggs and flour these are sweet, deep fried fritters dipped in sugary syrup. They are particularly popular during the rainy season.

Rasawal — Made with rice and sugarcane juice and simmered for hours in an earthenware pot, this dessert is prepared when the sugarcane is freshly cut. These days, *gur* is often used instead of sugarcane juice. It is served in semi-liquid form, usually as a dessert when *paya* are cooked, and is garnished with cream, nuts, raisins and desiccated coconut.

Goans

When Sir Charles Napier occupied Sindh in 1843, many Goan residents who did not want to live under Portuguese rule moved to Karachi, and were absorbed in the army as well as in civilian jobs. Some of them established bakeries which became extremely popular. To date there are bakeries in the Saddar area—where Goans had initially made their homes—that make Goan specialties, especially at Christmas and Easter. Goan cuisine generally draws on fish, coconut and rice, with chillies forming central ingredients. In fact, Goan dishes unite in their fiery sauces the culinary histories of three continents: Europe, Asia, and the Americas (Collingham 2006).

Breads

Saana — A spongy, white, slightly sweet, steamed coconut and rice bread, it is normally eaten with *sorpotel.*

Goan Specialties

Sorpotel — A dish of Portuguese origin it is made with pork elsewhere, but with mutton or beef in Pakistan. A special curry dish prepared on special occasions like Christmas, the meats are parboiled, diced and then sautéed before being cooked in spicy and vinegary sauce.

Kul kul — Made with eggs, sugar, flour and coconut milk, *kul kul* is a fried dessert that can be stored for days in an airtight container. It is often prepared ahead of Christmas.

Neureos — This is a tasty, sweet, deep fried patty made of flour, with coconut, cashew nuts and raisins filling.

Vindaloo — The term *vindaloo* is derived from the Portuguese dish 'Carne de Vinha d' Alhos' (Collingham 2006) traditionally made with pork preserved in red wine and chilli pepper, and stewed with garlic. It was first brought to Goa by the Portuguese and became a Goan meal often served on special occasions. It evolved into the *vindaloo* curry dish eaten in Pakistan when the Goans added plentiful spices to it and lots of vinegar.

Hot-cross buns — A hot-cross bun is a sweet yeast-leavened, spiced bun made with currants or raisins, often with candied citrus fruits, marked with a cross on top.

Anglo-Indians

The Anglo-Indians in Pakistan are the descendants of British or European men, generally from the colonial service or the military, and their Indian wives. After Partition, many opted to become Pakistanis, and settled mostly in urban centres, particularly Karachi. Some Anglo-Indian dishes include traditional British cuisine such as roast beef, but prepared with local spices minus ginger and coriander. However, while these have been adopted mostly by urban

Cutlets   Chicken patties

communities, there are many other British specialties adopted by the Anglo-Indians that have become as popular in small towns as in major cities.

Anglo-Indian Specialties

Mulligatawny soup — A thick, spicy chicken soup its basic ingredients today comprise pink lentils, rice, coconut milk, lemon juice and local spices. Although it is made in many different ways now, it usually has rice and chicken pieces floating in it.

An Anglo-Indian invention, *mulligatawny* soup is believed to have been created for the British Raj who demanded a soup course from a cuisine that had never produced one. The nearest dish to a soup that Madrassi cooks knew was a watery broth made from black pepper, tamarind and water called *molo tunny* in Tamil, or pepper water. The Madrassi cooks inventively added some rice, lentils, a few vegetables and little meat to the broth and transformed it into *mulligatawny* soup, one of the earliest dishes to emerge from the new hybrid cuisine (Collingham 2006).

According to a popular legend though, a district officer in the Punjab went for dinner to Malik Tiwana's house where he was served *daal chawal* and thoroughly enjoyed it. He returned home and asked his cook to conjure a similar dish. The concoction created was corrupted from *Malik Tiwana's* to *Mulligatawny*.

Cutlets — In Pakistani cuisine, cutlet specifically refers to cooked meat (minced mutton, beef, chicken or fish) or/and vegetable stuffing that is deep fried with a batter covering, usually of beaten eggs and breadcrumbs.

Patties — Made of pastry dough rolled out thinly, their characteristic flaky texture is achieved by repeatedly rolling out the dough, spreading it with butter and folding it to produce many thin layers of folds. Patties are light, airy and fatty, but firm enough to support the weight of the filling, which could be either mince meat (chicken or beef) or vegetable.

Bombay duck — While the British in Madras may have been responsible for the discovery of *mulligatawny*, the British in Bombay developed their area's specialty: bomelon—small fish

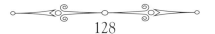

that the residents of Bombay treated with asafoetida, and then hung up to dry in the sun. Fried until they were golden-brown and sprinkled over food as a crunchy accompaniment, they imparted a strong, salty taste which the British loved. They christened this seasoning as *Bombay duck* as these fish were known to swim close to the surface of the water (Collingham 2006).

Desserts

Cakes — The ubiquitous plain cake, often consumed by dunking thick slices into piping hot tea is an all time favourite with Pakistanis of all classes and communities. However, the more exotic cakes with butter or cream icing and a variety of flavourings and toppings have become the rage primarily among the urban upper classes, and are popular items at tea parties.

Caramel custard/cream caramel — Introduced to the region by the Portuguese whose speciality was fragrant egg custard, a style of dessert entirely new to India (Collingham 2006), and a hot favourite with the British during colonial rule, this was one of the first desserts to be adopted by the local people who would call it *putin* as they couldn't pronounce *pudding*. With a caramelized sugar topping, caramel custard has milk, eggs and sugar as its ingredients. It is usually cooked in a double-broiler to ensure indirect heat, and baked in an oven.

Assorted cakes and pastries

Pastries — These are baked flour snacks made from ingredients such as flour, butter, sugar, shortening, baking powder and eggs. They include small cakes and tarts with a host of sweet fillings and toppings.

Biscuits — A hard, baked, small and flat sweet or savoury product, both handmade and machine-made biscuits are popular. They come in different textures and flavours, and like cakes, are often dunked in tea before being consumed.

Trifle — Made with a sponge cake base and layered with fruits, jelly and custard or cream, this dessert has become especially popular at Muslim weddings. A local variation is *lab-e-shireen*.

Gujaratis

Renowned for the simplicity of their lifestyle, Gujaratis are famous for their vegetarian cuisine. They are also known for a variety of snacks that have become particularly popular in Karachi. Gujaratis settled in Pakistan hail from various parts of India and their cuisine therefore, varies somewhat. Nonetheless, certain commonalities are to be found.

Breads

Bhakhri — Considered a complete meal on its own, this crispy, round, flat unleavened bread is made from *gehon*, *jowar* or *bajra* and is coarser than *chapati*.

Khakra — A tea-time snack, *khakra* is a popular, roasted crispy, crunchy paper-thin *chapati* made of whole wheat flour and oil. Added to it are different supporting ingredients such as *methi* and masala to make the *khakra* chunky.

Gujarati Specialties

Muthia — *Muthias*, so called because of the shape of the millet dumplings in this dish which look like a fist (*muthi* in Urdu)—is a winter specialty that includes assorted seasonal vegetables, mostly greens, and mutton. They are inspired by the Hindu *dhokri* except that this version also incorporates meat.

Khandvi — Made with chickpea flour, *bhoonoed* and flattened onto a *thaal*, *khandvi* is cut into strips, rolled and tempered with mustard seeds, asafoetida and sesame seeds.

Patherveli — There are several different ways of preparing this vegetarian delight. Made of layers of green vegetables and paste of chickpea flour, *patherveli* is commonly rolled up with spices and tamarind paste, and cut into slices and deep fried just prior to serving.

Mandazi — Typically an East African street food from the Swahili coastal areas, *mandazi* is a popular snack item that was adopted by Gujaratis settled there and brought to the places they later made their homeland. Similar to doughnuts, it is also eaten at breakfast, and often at lunch and dinner as a side item.

Papar — Also known as papadoms in the west, these are thin, round crisp tortillas, fried or roasted and served as an accompaniment to curries, *khichris*, etc.

Pawan matar-aloo bhaji — Flattened, boiled and dried rice, hydrated with water before cooking, *pawan* is stir-fried with potatoes and peas.

Kachoris — Many different forms of *kachoris* exist. Gujaratis generally make it as round balls of flour filled with a stuffing of *moong ki daal*, black pepper, red chilli powder and ginger paste. Other versions commonly found include *puris* stuffed with *moong ki daal* or *urad ki daal*, *besan*, ginger paste and red chilli powder, and served with *aloo ki bhaji*.

Pao bhaji — This is a square loaf of bread (*pao*) and vegetable curry (*bhaji*) dish. The vegetables are generally mixed—beans, carrots, cauliflowers, potatoes, bottle gourd, etc.

Kachoris

Bhel Puri

Desserts

Gundpak — A very nutritious dessert generally made in winter, it is often served to nursing mothers. Made with whole-wheat flour, jaggery, *gondh* (edible gum), almonds and milk it is cooked into a mixture and allowed to set on a greased baking tray, then cut into squares.

Gur paapri — Similar to *gundpak* but less sticky, this is a rich dessert also prepared in winter. It is basically made of whole-wheat flour, almonds, pistachios, poppy seeds, jaggery and edible gum and shaped into balls, or flattened and cut into diamonds.

Thepla — Deep fried sweet crisp *puris*, these are basically made with whole-wheat flour, eggs, jaggery, milk and butter. *Theplay* can be stored for days in airtight containers without going bad and are a popular tea-time snack.

Gajjak — *Gajjak* are dry, crunchy winter treats made of jaggery syrup and sesame seeds. The cooked mixture is allowed to set and then cut into squares.

Chikee — Caramelized almonds, cashew nuts or *chanay ki daal* these crunchy sweetmeats are mostly popular in winter, although available the year round.

Gur roti — Broken bits of *chapati*, these are mixed with melted *gur* and eaten warm.

Labsi — A delicious dessert of fried, coarsely-ground or broken wheat, it is cooked with milk, butter and sugar.

Sirkhan — This concentrated yogurt dish incorporates saffron and sugar.

Snacks

Bhel puri — This is a mouth watering tangy snack comprising puffed rice, lentils, chopped onions, potatoes, herbs, crisp fried pastry bits and two types of chutneys mixed together.

Pani puri — These are hollow, round, fried pastry shells filled with boiled chickpeas and served with a sweet-and-sour chutney.

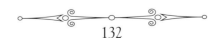

Items for Specific Occasions

Kantra — For the first few months after childbirth *kantra* is served to the nursing mother daily as it is believed to increase milk flow, and strengthen the back. Comprising dry fruits, herbs and gum cooked together, *kantra* is a nourishing source of energy normally consumed more in winter, when it is easier to digest this oil-rich food.

Doodh ka sherbet — A newly married couple is welcomed with *doodh ka sherbet* which is basically warm, saffron-infused sweetened milk with slivers of blanched almonds and pistachios.

While these dishes are common to practically all Gujaratis, there are certain dishes particularly associated with one or the other of the Gujarati-speaking communities settled in Pakistan—the Khojas, the Memons and the Bohras.

Khojas

Hailing originally from Kutch and Kathiawar in Gujarat, Khojas are a community that converted to Islam from Hinduism some five hundred years ago. Though mainly employed in business, Khojas are well known for producing professionals from several walks of life. Quaid-i-Azam Mohammad Ali Jinnah, the founder of the nation, himself was a Khoja.

Today, Khojas are to be found all over the world—East Africa, Madagascar, Pakistan, the Persian Gulf, the USA, Canada and Australia—and their cuisine differs substantially because of the varied influences of the countries in which they have settled. In Pakistan, for instance, there is a strong Mughal influence on many Khoja dishes. In fact, many food experts believe that Khoja cuisine is the best Mughlai cooking of all, for it incorporates the flavoursome meaty food of the Mughals with some interesting Gujarati influences. An exotic mixture of culinary styles, Pakistani Khoja cuisine includes delicately flavoured meat, fish and chicken dishes cooked with locally grown herbs and piquant home-ground masalas.

Having said that, there are some specialties that are typically associated with the Khoja community universally.

Khoja specialties

Among the most well-known Khoja dishes are:

Khichra — A sister of haleem, this is a dish made with ground wheat, four kinds of lentils, meat and spices. The wheat and lentils are cooked on low heat for seven to eight hours, all the while rigorously stirred, till it acquires a paste-like consistency and is ready to be served. The meat is cooked like a *qorma* and then mixed into the paste. A high-energy provider, it used to be cooked in *daigs* in the days of yore, to feed army camps.

Samosay — Inspired by the Tajik *sambusa* the Khoja version generally incorporates boiled minced meat or potatoes wrapped in a triangular-shaped very thin pastry that is deep fried rather than baked. Served in most communities as a snack item, it often constitutes a side dish in Khoja meals.

Samosay

Khichri — Various versions of this simple rice and lentil combination exist: from a dry version made with *moong ki daal* without skin, relished with fish or yogurt curry and eaten with papadoms, to an over-cooked, porridge-like version normally made with *moong ki daal* with the skin on, and eaten with plain yogurt, milk, or *achar*. If none of these accompaniments are available then it is eaten with green chutney or even *ghee*. This dish has been in existence from at least the fifteenth century and has been described in the writings of a Russian adventurer, Afanasy Nikitin, who travelled to the Indian subcontinent in the fifteenth century. In fact, the Mughal Emperor Jehangir is believed to have sampled this Gujarati favourite while travelling through the province of Gujarat and finding that it suited him a lot, ordered his people to serve it to him on his vegetarian days, thus integrating it into the Mughlai repertoire (Collingham 2006).

Daal gosht with meethay chawal — Made with a combination of four *daals*—*chana, moong, masoor* and *arhar*— boiled together and mixed with meat curry, this dish is uniquely enough, often eaten with sweetened rice (*zerda*).

Ghatia salan — Made in the traditional style of *gosht ka salan* by frying onions and *bhunoing* masalas in it before adding meat and water, the only difference in this curry-based dish is that *ghatia* (fried strips of *besan* dough) are added in it.

Anday ka qeema — Made with beaten eggs, onions, potatoes and tomatoes cut fine, and with a *baghar* of cumin seeds or mustard seeds this is a *desi* version of scrambled eggs that can be had at any meal.

Anday wala khana — A rice-based dish which incorporates *chanay ki daal* or *arhar ki daal* cooked in masala, with boiled eggs that have been lightly fried, and potatoes added to it, it is made with the gravy mixture placed in a layer over the boiled rice, before being put on *dum*.

Methi anda — This delicious egg curry consists of boiled eggs simmered in yogurt, spices and fresh fenugreek leaves.

Gosht ki kari — This dish incorporates parboiled mutton cooked in lots of ground masala including *til* (sesame seeds), *khaskhas* (poppy seeds), *mung phalli* (peanuts), roasted gram and cashew nuts, roasted and ground onions, and tamarind. It is normally eaten with *baghara hua* (lightly fried) rice or *double roti*.

Bombay biryani — The spiciest of all the different kinds of *biryanis* made in Pakistan, *Bombay biryani* consists of alternate layers of boiled rice, and lamb or chicken and potato gravy. It is usually eaten in accompaniment with *kachumer*.

Dahi ki kari — Made with yogurt, preferably a little sour, and *besan* paste, this tangy curry has a history that dates back to the twelfth century, and has been described by the Hindu King Somesvara III [who ruled over parts of present-day Maharashtra and Karnataka] (Collingham 2006) in his book *Manasollasa*. With deep fried fritters of *besan* floating in it, it is normally eaten with *bhoonni khichri* (the drier version of *khichri*), *papar* and *achar*.

Lassan — Made with *hara lassan* (garlic chives) and *bajray ki roti* mashed together, lightly seasoned, smoked, and then made into balls with lots of desi ghee, this is a winter favourite when *lassan* is in season, and is eaten normally for breakfast. *Bhurta* made with yogurt and smoked eggplant is normally served as an accompaniment.

Masoor pulao — This meat *pulao* is made with *masoor ki daal* with the skin on and which has been pre-soaked in water, rice, boiled eggs, and potatoes. Often minced meat is also added to the dish.

Aloo chaap — Various versions exist, but traditionally *aloo chaap* is a cutlet made with mashed potatoes with a minced meat filling. Quite deceptively named!

Naan chaap — This is a dry mince dish accompanied with *naan*.

Bombay Biryani

Malpuray

Half gosht — Unlike most meat curry dishes, this mutton and *chanay ki daal* dish is made with *bhoonna* process taking place after adding the meat rather than in the beginning of cooking.

Desserts

Malpuray — These sweet pancakes made out of flour, milk, sugar, eggs and red pumpkin are fried and served with full cream. Particularly popular in Ramazan, in recent years, it has become a popular dessert at weddings where *malpuray* are fried at the site.

Ghas ka halwa — This dessert is supposed to have a cooling effect, and hence is particularly popular in summer. Made with china grass that has been soaked and then boiled in water, the only other main ingredient used in it is sugar.

Aam ka rus aur puri — A summer favourite, particularly among mango fans, this dish comprises mango pulp blended with milk and sugar into a thick shake, and small puris.

Bohras

Bohras are a Shia Muslim community that originates from Gujarat, India. They trace their conversion to Islam from Hinduism in approximately AD 1100 when Arab Ismaili missionaries arrived from Yemen to Gujarat. The word Bohra (also spelled 'Vohra') is derived from the Gujarati word *vohorvu* or *vyavahar* which means 'to trade'. As the name indicates, the community comprised primarily traders, as is the case even today.

Traditionally, Bohras eat communally from large *thaals* which are steel platters holding several *katoris* or small bowls, each one filled with a different item. The dining etiquette for eating from a *thaal* requires a minimum of seven people to be seated around it while it is normally placed on the floor on a steel ring called *kundli*. The floor is covered with a large printed cloth called *jazam* over which is placed a square cotton cloth called *safro* in the centre of which is placed the ring. Diners sit around the *thaal* on the *safro*, their legs tucked under the raised *thaal* and eat directly off it. However, the *thaal's* popularity among non-Bohras has resulted in a modernized version of it, with the *thaal* often placed on top of a dining table and diners serving themselves from it in plates. Typically, the meal is initiated with a pinch of salt, followed by a sweet dish and then the main course, ending with a dessert. Today, eating out of *thaals*, even among many Bohras, is reserved for special occasions.

Another aspect of Bohra cuisine is that unlike most Pakistani foods which are made with hot spices, Bohra cuisine has a base of green masala—made with ginger, garlic and green chillies ground together—and hence, is lighter on the palate. Another interesting culinary-related fact about Bohras is that they do not eat fish unless it has been caught by one of their own, as they feel that fish too, should be halal. And they only eat fish with scales. *Dhungar* is often given to dishes to give them an irresistible, smoky flavour.

Bohra Specialties

Daal chawal palidu — Normally served at dinner on festive occasions, this dish is part of the *thaal* feast that Bohras partake of as a thanksgiving celebration. The *palidu* comprises gourd (*doodhi*) cooked with onions, masala, gram flour and mangostein until it becomes a thick paste. It is eaten with cooked *arhar ki daal* and boiled rice, layered alternately.

Cutless — These are cutlets made with uncooked mince and bread, coated with breadcrumbs and egg before being deep fried. They are often called *jaali wallay kebab* by non-Bohras, because of their net-like appearance.

Moong salad — Rarely made by any other community, this *moong* bean salad is made of roasted *moong* beans, boiled and cubed potatoes and shredded cabbage, mixed with tamarind chutney and yogurt and topped with a *baghar*.

Pickles — Unlike the pickles generally made by other communities, Bohra pickles are not oil-based, but vinegar or lemon-based. The popular ones are of carrot, lemon, mixed vegetables and raw mango.

Dhokra — Another version of the Hindu *dhokri* and the Khoja *muthia*, the Bohra *dhokray* are also made of assorted vegetables and millet dumplings. The only difference between

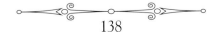

Vinegar-based pickles

this and the other two dishes is that the Bohra *dhokra* also includes mince and drumsticks as opposed to no meat at all in *dhokri*, and mutton in *muthia*.

Haleem — The Bohra *haleem* is different from the Hyderabadi *haleem* in that no pulses are incorporated and it is made purely from wheat and mashed meat that has been boiled. Traditionally, the Bohra *haleem* is eaten with *bharta*, a combination of yogurt and eggplant, and *kaddi*, a tangy, yogurt-based curry, and *karak roti* (hard loaf of bread).

Curry chawal — Similar in some ways to the Khoja *gosht ki kari* in that it is made with more or less the same masala, this curry incorporates cream of coconut and no onions.

Lagan seekh — Basically meat loaf, it is made with mince meat, eggs, potatoes, and onions mixed together, patted into a tray, and baked in an oven.

Gosh nu saag — The difference between this meat curry and the ones normally made in the country—aside from the fact that it has a green curry base—is that most ingredients in this curry, including onions, are left partially uncooked before the meat is added to it. In most meat curries the ingredients are fried (through the process of *bhoonnoing*) before the meat and water is added.

Maggio — Made with boiled rice layered over boiled *moong ki daal* that has been cooked with yogurt, onions, tomatoes and spices, this dish is prepared through the *dum* technique of cooking.

Daal ka hasma — *Hasma* means mixture, so any mixture of food constitutes *hasma*. It is usually made of leftovers—at the end of a meal all leftover food in the *thaal* is mixed together into a *hasma* in order to ensure everything is eaten, to prevent wastage. *Daal hasma* is made of leftover *chapati* and rice mixed with *daal* of liquid consistency (made from mixing three *daals*—chana, *moong* and *masoor*). The mixture is then smoked to give added flavour.

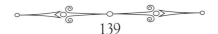

Other food items such as leftover meat and gravy, freshly cut onions and tomatoes or *achar* can also be added to the *daal hasma*.

Khatia — This Bohra version of shepherd's pie is made of leftover *biryani*, yogurt and masala cooked into a paste.

Braise — Braise is actually a Gujarati distortion of 'breast', and comprises mutton ribs. Boiled in *hara masala* and then given *baghar*, usually of just black pepper, it is considered one of the best cuts of meat and is often served to in-laws at weddings.

Desserts

Malai khaja — This rich puff-pastry filled with *mawa*, dry fruits and cottage cheese is often distributed on special occasions like engagements and weddings.

Churma ladwa — These are *ladoos* (a dessert in the shape of balls) basically made with semolina, brown flour, milk and sugar and enriched with almonds, pistachio and saffron.

Gundh phera — Made with edible gum, whole-wheat flour, sugar and *ghee*, and enriched with pistachios, almonds, cardamom and saffron, this crumb-like dessert is particularly popular in winter and regarded as a highly nourishing dish for young mothers.

Malai Khaja

Malido — Made with fried and crushed whole-wheat flour, butter, edible gum, jaggery, almonds and pistachios, this is another rich dessert popular in winter.

Damido/Anday ka mesu — This is an egg *halwa* made with *ghee*, sugar and evaporated milk.

Doodhi falooda — Made with grated gourd, cream and milk, this dessert is served cold.

Karmo — Made of boiled and mashed rice, jaggery and yogurt, this simple dessert is garnished with crushed almonds and pistachios.

Soufflé — Bohras are famous for their soufflés which are inspired by the traditional English soufflés, but made differently from them. Using ice-cold, whipped evaporated milk, jelly and fruits, all mixed together, this dessert is chilled for two to three hours before serving.

Kharak — Made especially on Eid to serve guests, *kharak* is dried *khajoor* slit lengthwise from the centre, de-seeded, and soaked in sugar syrup for a couple of hours. It is then filled with a rich mixture of powdered dry fruit and sugar and served to all visiting guests on Eid-ul-Fitr.

Sundhera — A dish served on *Pehli Raat* or the eve of Moharram, this is sweet rice made by boiling rice and mixing it with sugar and warm *ghee*. It is garnished with almonds and pistachios. It is served as a starter in a *thaal* on special occasions, to be taken after the pinch of salt. *Sundhera* is offered in a very small plate; the objective being that each person sitting around the *thaal* gets a small bite.

Memons

Majority of Memons in Pakistan trace their roots either to Kutch or Kathiawar. However, there is one school of thought that believes they originated from Thatta in Sindh. The converts, they opine were first called 'Momins' and the term subsequently evolved into 'Memons'.

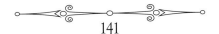

Memon Specialties

Akhni — Unlike most *pulaos* this rice dish is made in red masala and not green, and the mutton and rice are cooked with red chillies. Turmeric is also used, so the rice is yellow in colour.

Dhokri wali kari — Made like the normal *dahi ki kari*, this one does not have *pakoray* in it. Instead, *dhokris*—made from *besan* and boiling water, and cut into pieces after setting in a pan—is immersed in it. The *kari* is eaten with *khichri*.

Daal baray — Made with ground lentils soaked for a few hours and then mixed with chopped onions, tomatoes and spices, and shaped into *baray*, these crispy delicacies are fried deftly on a *tawa* with very little oil.

Dhokray — Yet another variation of the Hindu *dhokri*, this dish also incorporates a variety of vegetables and fist-shaped rolls made of *bajra*. The difference between this dish and its other versions is that the Memon *dhokra* normally has fish instead of mutton.

Akhni

142

Desserts

Monthal — This gram-flour dessert is made with condensed milk, sugar syrup and milk, and garnished with pistachios and almonds. It is allowed to set in a greased pan and cut into squares before serving.

Parsis

When the Zoroastrians fled from Persia (mainly from the province of Pars) over a thousand years ago to escape religious persecution, they were given asylum in Gujarat, and settled in Surat (Monier-Williams 2000) where they eventually came to be known as Parsis or 'people of Pars'. Although they assimilated with the local population, adopting the language and attire of their Hindu benefactors, they maintained their distinct identity. Their food, blended with Indian influences, produced a distinctive cuisine that is universal in taste. By the middle of the nineteenth century, Parsis had settled in Karachi in substantial numbers, retaining a great deal of their ancient heritage in their religious and gastronomical habits. However, although most Parsis adhere strictly to Zoroastrianism, they are one of the most westernised of all Pakistani communities. As such they have hardly any food restrictions and their cuisine is a delicious blend of sweet and sour flavours.

Parsi Specialties

Akoori — A famous breakfast dish of the Parsis, it is just as welcome at any meal. Basically scrambled eggs cooked with onions and tomatoes, it is served on toast.

Dhansak — This is a robust dish containing meat, pureed lentils—sometimes up to six types are used—vegetables, including eggplant, pumpkin, potatoes and tomatoes—and spices. It has a unique spicy, sweet and tangy flavour. It is traditionally served with browned rice, especially on Ghambar, a thanksgiving feast. However, other than on Ghambar, *dhansak* is normally cooked on sad occasions and is not regarded as a celebratory food.

Patia — *Patia* is a traditional Parsi dish that was brought from Persia by Parsis who settled in Tarapore, now in Gujarat. It is made with prawns or fish, cooked with spices, herbs, jaggery or palm sugar and tamarind. Chicken or lamb versions also exist but are not originally Parsi. It is usually served on special occasions like birthdays, weddings or any auspicious occasion like Navroz—marking the beginning of the Persian year and the advent of spring, celebrated on 21 March—with *arhar daal* and boiled rice. This spicy, sweet and sour dish can be eaten hot or cold and can be stored in the refrigerator in an air-tight jar for up to a month.

Patarani machli — A favourite dish served at Parsi weddings, it comprises fish (sole, plaice or pomfret) cut in slices, covered with grated coconut chutney, and wrapped individually in banana leaves that have been softened over fire. The pieces are then fried until the leaves turn dark and the fish is cooked within. Some prefer to steam or bake the fish rather than fry it.

Jardaloo ma gos — This mutton dish is cooked like regular curry except that no tomatoes or yogurt is added to it. Instead, dried apricots soaked in water overnight and par-boiled are essential ingredients. Fried potatoes are added to the half-cooked mutton and simmered until the meat becomes tender.

Dhan dar machli — This boiled white rice dish served with plain *tarka daal* is accompanied with *patia*. The served rice is first topped with two or three tablespoons of *daal* and further topped with a tablespoon of *patia*.

Sookha boomla nu tarapori patio — This is a specialty of the Parsis of Tarapore, and is made with dried Bombay duck. These are fried in masala, onions and vinegar, and can be eaten hot or cold. It can be stored in an air-tight jar for up to a month in the refrigerator. When left dry, it is served as a pickle, and when cooked in slightly liquid form, it is eaten with *khichree*.

Khara papeta ma gosht — Similar to the *gosht ka salan* or *aloo gosht* normally consumed all over the country, the difference is that this Parsi mutton dish is cooked only in onions and whole spices and no tomatoes or yogurt is added.

Desserts

Rava — Eaten generally at breakfast on festive occasions as an alternate to *sheerkhurma*, this sweet dish is made of semolina, and flavoured with rosewater or garnished with rose petals.

Malido — Made with flour, wheat flour and semolina cooked in *ghee* and milk, and then mixed with sugar syrup, eggs, almonds and cashew nuts, this Parsi sweet dish can be stored in the refrigerator for a month. It is eaten hot or at room temperature.

Sheedis

Like the Makranis, Sheedis are of African descent. It is probable that they were an ethnic group of Sidama origin from southern Ethiopia from which many were sold into slavery mainly by local traders. However, there are linguistic indications also that show that they were predominantly Swahili speaking people (Yimene 2004). Recurring famine brought them liberty and today, the largest community of Sheedis exists in Sindh. The cuisine of Sheedis is similar to that of the Makranis. Those settled in Karachi prefer to eat *roti* for lunch and rice at night. They are fond of eating dried fish which they scramble and cook like curry.

Chinese

During the 1940s many Chinese Muslims fled unrest in China and settled in Karachi. However, currently, the Chinese community here is primarily of non-Muslim origin — their ancestors were Buddhists, but subsequent generations followed other religions or none at all. About thirty per cent are estimated to have converted to Islam. Most Chinese in Karachi are second generation children of immigrants—most of the oldest generation having passed away—while the third generation has migrated to other countries.

Chinese cuisine in Pakistan has been adapted to suit Pakistani tastes, incorporating Pakistani seasonings and techniques of cooking and doing away with some authentic

Chinese ingredients. So popular have these dishes become that even restaurants specialising in Pakistani cuisine have Chinese dishes on their menu! However, there are certain Chinese dishes that are patronized by the Chinese community which have not become popular with locals, such as *jiaozi* (also known as *gau gee*). These are steamed dumplings made with thinly rolled dough boasting vegetable or minced meat filling. It is particularly popular at the Chinese New Year. Another specialty that few Pakistanis have acquired a taste for but remains a favourite with the Chinese is *dim sum*—small individual portions of food usually served in a steamer basket.

Chinese Specialties

Chicken fried rice — Comprising boiled rice that is stir-fried with finely chopped vegetables such as carrots, peas and spring onions, boiled and shredded chicken and cooked eggs, this dish is a complete meal on its own.

Chicken corn soup — A popular soup that has been adopted so widely by the population that it is even sold at wayside stalls on the streets of Karachi this broth is made with sweet corn, shredded chicken and cornflour.

Chow mein — Made with boiled egg noodles stir fried with shredded and marinated chicken, and vegetables, this is a light dish that is often eaten on its own.

Chicken Corn Soup

Spring rolls — A very popular side item that has been incorporated in local snacks, spring rolls are crispy fried rolls stuffed with stir-fried vegetables.

Bengali

The influence of East Bengal, a part of Pakistan till 1971, is most noticeable in the desserts which have been adopted by the local gastronomy and have become extremely popular, particularly in Karachi, where Dhaka-based sweetmeat shops have established branches.

Bengali Desserts

Rasgullay — *Rasgullay* are among the most favourite Bengali sweets, comprising spongy balls basically made of milk powder soaked in lightly sweet sugar syrup. *Sandesh*, supposedly a predecessor of *rasgullay* is a lot less sweet, and has not gained as much favour with the general populace as *rasgullay*, although, *sandesh* is available at certain sweet meat shops here. In fact, it was because of *sandesh's* limited popularity, that according to a legend, Nobin Chandra Sen, a late nineteenth century sweet maker, not content with serving his patrons the traditional plain sweet, experimented with boiling a *sandesh* in syrup, and invented the *rasgulla*.

Rasmalai — Similar to *rasgullay*, *rasmalai* is immersed in sweetened cooked milk and not in sugar syrup.

Sandesh — Similar to *rasgullay* but not as sweet, the texture of *sandesh* is soft and dry. It is not immersed in sweetened syrup.

Meethi dahi — Made and served in clay containers (*kulias*) this is basically sweetened yogurt made by boiling and fermenting milk and sugar overnight and adding curd.

Rasmalai

Others

Lebanese

Shawarma — This Lebanese specialty is made by roasting a cone of pressed lamb, chicken or beef on a vertical spit. The meat is shaved off from the outside as the spit keeps turning, and is then sandwiched within *khubbs* (Arabic bread) along with fresh and pickled vegetables, hot sauce and tahina.

Shawerma

Khow Suey

Burmese

Khows Suey — A Burmese specialty, it is an elaborate dish comprising boiled noodles, coconut-based curry, meat curry (made with bite-size undercut pieces) and condiments including boiled eggs, lime, fried noodles, fried garlic and onions. Variations of this dish are made using chicken instead of undercut, and by combining the two curries into one. Even the condiments vary depending on taste.

Japanese, Thai, Italian and American

Japanese, Thai, Italian and American cuisine have gained popularity in urban Karachi and to an extent in Lahore and Islamabad, where niche restaurants have opened up specializing in international cuisine. While not many can afford to frequent Japanese and Thai restaurants, Italian eateries, particularly pizza joints, and American fast-food franchise restaurants serving burgers have become household names as much in middleclass families as in the elite classes.

Sheesha

While not a food item, *sheesha* warrants some mention. Originating from Arabia, it has, in recent years, become a hot favourite with everybody, regardless of their age or gender. Similar to our *huqqa* that has been part of our village culture for centuries; *sheesha* is also essentially a pipe with a water-filter for smoking tobacco leaves or dry fruit.

11

Snacks for All Occasions

Considered a luxury item snacks are regularly eaten in a large number of households in the bigger cities, where the more affluent families, regardless of their ethnic backgrounds, normally partake of them with their evening tea. They also serve as cheap, quick filler-meals for many. Popular savoury snack items include *samosay*, crisps, french fries, sandwiches, *pakoray*, *shami kebabs*, *nimco*, cake and biscuits. *Chaats* such as *aloo cholay*, *dahi baray* and fruit *chaat* are also hot favourites universally. In winters, dry fruits (almonds, walnuts, pine nuts, currants and cashew nuts) also constitute as popular snack items. Sweet snacks such as *mithai* and cakes are generally not as popular as the savoury ones.

Samosay — *Samosa* has been a popular snack in the subcontinent for centuries. It is believed that it originated in Central Asia (where they are known as *samsa*, while they are called *sambusa* in Tajikistan) prior to the tenth century. In Pakistan, it generally consists of a crispy, fried, triangular shaped dough wafer with a choice of savoury filling—spiced potatoes, minced meat, chicken or fresh *paneer* (cottage cheese).

Pakoray — Made with a paste of gram flour and water mixed with spices and onions or a host of other vegetables such as eggplant, potatoes and spinach, deep fried hot *pakoray* are a great favourite particularly in Ramazan, and during the rainy season.

Pakoray

Kachoris — *Puris* stuffed with pulses, *kachoris* are often eaten with potato *bhujia*.

Bun kebabs — A local version of burgers, *bun kebabs* are available at roadside kiosks and push-carts known as *thailas*. The patty is either of beef or of potato together with *chanay ki daal*, and is generally topped with egg, vegetables and an assortment of chutneys.

Chaats

Chaat, an Indic word which literally means 'lick', is used to describe a range of snacks and fast-food dishes comprising assorted savouries such as *tikkis*, *chana paapri* (chickpeas with crispy fried dough wafers), *golgappe* (hollow, fried crisp *puris* also known as *pani puris*), *masalai wallay aloos* (spicy potatoes), and mixed fruits with *chaat masala*, dished out with sweet and sour chutneys and tangy sprinklers. Popular ones include:

Chana chaat — It is believed that during the reign of the Mughal Emperor Mohammad Shah (AD 1719–48), *chaat* became a rage when the court hakim recommended highly spiced dishes to keep stomach problems and germs at bay. Today, *chana chaat*—a concoction of boiled chickpeas, potatoes, finely sliced green chillies, onions and tomatoes, topped with tamarind chutney, sweet chutney, spicy yogurt and *chaat masala*—is one of the most popular snacks one can partake of.

Chana Chaat

Paapri chaat — A slight variation of *chana chaat*, *paapri* refers to crispy fried dough wafers made from refined white flour and oil. In *paapri chaat*, the *paapris* are served with boiled potatoes, boiled chickpeas, chillies, yogurt and tamarind chutney, and topped with *chaat masala*. The *paapri* provides the *chaat* with a crunchiness that enhances the flavour.

Dahi baray/dahi bhalley/dahi vada — A sweet and sour snack, this item comprises spongy, deep fried lentil dumplings immersed in smoothly beaten yogurt, and sprinkled with *chaat masala* and tamarind chutney. It is believed to be a variation of an ancient dish from Dravidian times in South India, called *vartaka* which was made of beans, soaked overnight and then skinned before being pounded and deep fried.

Dahi Baray

Paapri

Fruit Chaat

Fruit chaat — Made of mixed fruits, particularly guavas, grapes, tangerines and pomegranate, and seasoned with sugar, cinnamon powder and *chaat masala*, this snack item possesses a refreshing tangy-sweet taste. When incorporating just guavas and ripe bananas, it is referred to as *kutchaloos*.

Pani puri — *Pani puri* or *gol gappa* is a popular street snack item in Pakistan. The name *pani puri* literally means 'water in fried bread'. It comprises crispy fried, round, hollow *puris* which are filled with boiled chickpeas and then dipped in a watery mixture of tamarind and chillies and a few other spices.

Bhel puri — *Bhelpuri* was originally a Gujarati fast-food item. Even amongst *chaat* experts, there is much disagreement as to what goes into a genuine *bhel puri*. Now, it is usually made according to consumer/producer preference, and the availability of ingredients. Most recipes include puffed rice *sev,* (a fried snack made from *besan* flour) and onions. Diced, boiled potatoes form the base of the snack, topped with different chutneys. There are two popular chutneys used: a dark purple sweet one made mainly of dates and tamarind, and a spicy green chutney made of ground coriander leaves.

Dum aloo — These became popular in the grand Mughal courts, employing the *dum* technique of cooking. Mughals did not eat too many vegetables and among the few they did eat were potatoes, often cooked slowly and gently in a thick, dark sauce.

Nimco — A classic example of how the widespread popularity of a product has turned its brand name into a generic one, *nimco* is a term widely used to describe a large variety of munchies including chilly and plain crisps, chilly and salted peanuts, *chewra* (puffed rice mixed with peanuts), *crispy moong ki daal*, *chanay ki daal*, *ghatia* (fried strips of *besan* dough) and much more. The first outlet to sell these delicious snacks by the name of 'Nimco' was established by Haji Muhammad Jan in the early 1950s.

Gola ganda — A popular summer favourite, *gola ganda* is a delightful concoction of shaved ice mixed with coloured syrups, fruit and condensed milk (optional). It is served either as a popsicle or in a cup, and is normally sold on push-carts on streets.

Pani Puri

12

Special Occasions and Traditional Dishes

Generous hospitality is the hallmark of the traditional fabric of Pakistan. The value of guests is immense: they are offered the best, and meals served to them are a matter of honour for the host. The cost of the dish is often overlooked on these occasions, and extra time and care are devoted to cooking them. Hence, the menu for special occasions is usually not the same as for everyday meals. This trend holds true across almost all ethnic groups. A variety of dishes are cooked on a special-occasion meal, which also includes a few specialties, and is always topped with a dessert.

Ramazan

The ninth month of the Islamic calendar, Ramazan is a month of fasting and abstinence meant to cleanse one's body and soul. Two meals are normally eaten throughout the month: one before dawn—this meal is known as *sehri*—and the other at sunset, known as *iftari*. While personal choices prevail as to what one eats at the two meals, there are certain dishes that are traditionally linked to each of these meals, and a large number of households partake of them.

Sehri — *Parathay*, eggs, mince meat, *jalebi* soaked in milk (a pretzel-shaped fried sweet made from white flour), *pheni* (vermicelli) soaked in milk, *khaja* (crisp wafers) and tea are among the items most likely to grace a table set for *sehri*. In recent years *sehri* parties have become popular amongst the elite, and on such occasions a lavish spread is laid out for the guests.

Sheerkhurma

Iftari — Traditionally, a fast is broken at *iftari* with dates or salt, after which all kinds of snack items followed by main meal dishes are consumed. For *iftar* it is the norm to find *pakoray*, *chaat* items, particularly *fruit chaat*, and *mithai* such as *jalebi* on the table. *Rooh-e-Afza*, a refreshing syrup mixed with water or milk, is another favourite in most households.

Eid-ul-Fitr

Also known as Ramazan Eid, this festive event follows Ramazan. To mark the occasion, special desserts of *sewayian* (vermicelli) and *sheerkhurma*—vermicelli in cooked milk—are prepared first thing in the morning in most homes and served to all visitors.

Eid-ul-Azha or Baqra Eid

This is a festive, religious occasion to commemorate Prophet Ibrahim's (Abraham) readiness to obey God's commandment—to the extent of even willing to sacrifice his son. It is also one of the last rites of the Hajj. Goats, lambs, cows and camels are symbolically sacrificed on Eid-ul-Azha by Muslims in great numbers, and the meat is distributed amongst relatives, the poor and the needy; while a portion is kept by the household to cook special dishes. Not surprisingly, barbecued mutton and beef are the order of the day and are served in conjunction with other exotic meat items such as *biryani* and *qorma*.

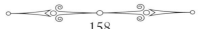

Navroz

Jamshed Peshdadiyan, one of the most illustrious kings of the Peshdadiyan dynasty of ancient Iran, founded the festival of Navroz (new day in Persian) to be celebrated on 21 March, heralding the bounties of spring after the barrenness of winter. Today, Navroz is celebrated by people influenced by Iranian culture, notably the Zoroastrians (Parsis), the Bahais, the Ismailis, and the Kurds. In fact, Navroz is unique in the sense that it is the only holiday celebrated by more than one religious community.

Among the best known Parsi traditions of Navroz is the *sofreh haft-seen*, or tablecloth with seven items beginning with the Persian alphabet *seen*, which symbolizes new beginnings. These are generally: *samanu*—a sweet pudding made from wheat germ, representing wealth; *seer*—garlic, symbolizing health; *saib*—apple, representing beauty; *somaq*—special berries symbolizing the colour of the sunrise; *serkeh*—vinegar, representing maturity and patience; *sumbul*—the hyacinth flower with its strong fragrance, heralding the coming of spring; and *sekkeh*—coins symbolizing prosperity and wealth.

A week or so before the holiday, grains of wheat and lentils are placed in bowls to sprout into a mass of greens, signifying growth. The table is also arranged with fruits, nuts, sweets and snacks (to herald a plentiful year), candles, a photograph of Zarathushtra, and a copy of the Avesta, the holy book of the Zoroastrians. A bowl with goldfish and a basket of coloured eggs kept replenished for thirteen days, indicating new life, are also placed on the table.

Custom dictates that visitors on Navroz should be sprinkled with rosewater, have a red dot (*tilli*) placed on their forehead, and be asked to look into a mirror to make a wish. Some say that these rituals signify 'smelling as sweet as roses' and 'shining as bright as a mirror' throughout the New Year.

Shab-e-Barat

Shab-e-Barat (All Souls Day) is celebrated culturally by preparing *halwa* of any kind—of pulses, vegetables, dates, semolina, etc.—and sharing it with family, friends, and neighbours.

Deep fried Pakoray   Gulgulay

Rainy Days

Since rainy days are few and far between in Pakistan, they are welcomed with great fervour, and looked upon as a reason for rejoicing—and what better way to rejoice than with food! *Pakoray* are a universal favourite and the onset of a shower is almost invariably followed by the family celebrating by partaking of hot *pakoray* and chutney. *Chaats* are also extremely popular in the rainy season. *Gulgulay*—similar to small dumplings, but richer and sweeter—*jalebis*, and *amirti* are popular dessert items in this season, and consumed fresh and hot. In Balochistan, *meethay parathay* or *meethi roti* is especially prepared using *gur* to welcome the rains.

Ashura

Haleem and *khichra*, although popular dishes round the year, are particularly associated with Ashura, the tenth day of Muharram (the first month of the Islamic calendar), marking the martyrdom of Imam Hussain—grandson of the Prophet (PBUH)—his family and compatriots. In commemoration, many Muslims spend this day in fasting and worship. The fast is usually broken with either *haleem* or *khichra*, both of which are high-energy givers. Believed to have been introduced to the subcontinent by Persians, *haleem* has several variations, and in Anatolia, Iran, Northern Iraq and the Caucasus region is known as *keshkek* and *harisa*. However, *haleem* basically comprises meat and whole-wheat and may or may not include pulses, while *khichra* incorporates four kinds of pulses, whole-wheat and meat.

Koonday Ki Niaz

The seventh month of the Islamic year, Rajab is a month of *niaz*. Traditionally, friends and relatives are invited to partake of *kheer* and *puri* that have been cooked as a dedication to Imam Jaffer Sadiq, the sixth *imam*—a direct descendent of Prophet Muhammad (PBUH). Often silver rings are mixed into the *kheer* and it is believed that those who find them when pouring out the *kheer* into their bowls will have a lucky year.

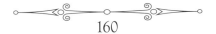

Lab-e-Shireen

Weddings

While different regions have their own specialties which they serve at weddings, by and large *biryani* and *qorma* are regarded as standard wedding fare practically throughout the country. A barbecued or fried item often accompanies the main dishes, while for dessert, generally depending on the season, there is a choice of *gajar ka halwa*, *loki ka halwa*, *gulab jaman*, *jaleebi*, *kulfi*, trifle or *lab-e-shireen*.

At mehendis, the festive occasion prior to the wedding revolving around song-and-dance, the menu is normally barbecue—*seekh kebab* and/or *chicken boti*—and *paratha*, along with *aloo ki bhujia* and *kachori*.

Fateha

Daal gosht or *kadoo wali daal* and plain boiled rice is traditionally served after funeral prayers to all present at the home of the deceased, though again, it varies from family to family, and sometimes the fare could include *qorma*.

Christmas

The Christian community settled in the country, particularly the Punjabi Christians, celebrates the birth of Christ in much the same way as Muslims celebrate Eid. Dessert in the form of *sewayian*, *kheer*, *neuri* and *goja* (made from semolina and dry fruits), custard or cake is prepared to be shared with friends and family.

Easter

Like in the west, Easter eggs made out of chocolate shells are popular with the Christian community.

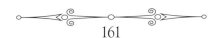

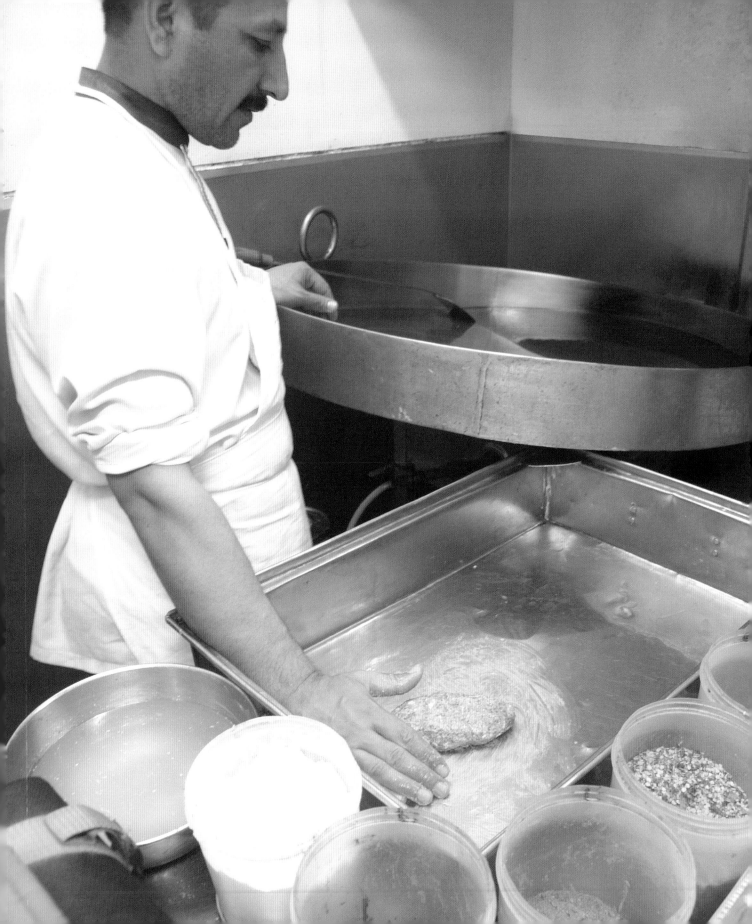

13

The Author's Favourite Pakistani Recipes

Chapli Kebab

Ingredients

Minced beef — ½ kg
Coriander seeds (coarsely ground) — 2 tbsp
Whole red chillies — 1½ tbsp
Pomegranate seeds — 1 tbsp
Gram flour — 2 tbsp
Cumin — 1 tsp
Hot spices powder — ½ tbsp
Chopped onions — 2
Eggs — 3–4
Ground ginger — ½ tsp
Ground garlic — ½ tsp
Oil — to fry
Salt — to taste

Method

Soak whole red chillies in water; remove seeds and grind coarsely. Mix well all ingredients with mince and keep aside for at least an hour. Shape into big, round kebabs and fry on a *tawa*.

Chicken Tikka Pizza

Ingredients

For dough:

Flour — 1¾ lb.

Water — 6 oz

Oil — 3 tbsp

Warm water—as required

Yeast — 20 g

Sugar — 1 tsp

Salt — 1 tsp

For sauce:

Tomatoes — 6

Oregano — ½ tsp

Onions — 2 (chopped)

Salt and pepper to taste

For Chicken Tikka:

Chicken cubes (boneless) — 1 kg

Turmeric — ½ tbsp

Red chilli powder — 1 tsp

Black pepper — ½ tsp

Oil – 2 tbsp

Salt — ½ tsp

Lemon juice — 2 tbsp

Ginger/garlic paste — 1 tsp

Mixed spices powder — 1 tsp

Nutmeg/mace — ½ tsp

For topping:

Onion — 1 (cubed)

Cheddar cheese — 1 cup (grated)

Mozzarella cheese — 2 cups (grated)

Method

Dissolve yeast in a tall container with 1 part boiling water and 3 parts cold water and place the container in a bowl of hot water. Add sugar and leave aside in a closed place for at least 15 minutes, till the yeast rises. Mix yeast in flour; add salt and oil and knead dough using warm water. Knead dough for 10 minutes, stretching it constantly. Press it down with thumb to see if it rises; if it does, the dough is ready. Oil it; cover with a wet cloth and keep in the sun or in a warm place for 30 minutes. Pat the dough and leave aside again for 30 minutes.

Boil tomatoes for few seconds; peel. Fry onions till golden; add tomatoes. Season with salt, pepper and oregano. Cook till water dries and remove from flame when puree is thick. Make cuts on chicken pieces and marinate with all tikka ingredients; set aside for 2–3 hours. Bake in over at 180°C for 30 minutes and smoke with charcoal. Roll out dough and set in pizza pans. Prick with fork. Spread sauce, cheddar cheese, chicken pieces, onion and mozzarella cheese. Bake in pre-heated oven at 250°C for 15 minutes.

Pasanday

Ingredients

Beef pasanday (undercut) — 2 lb.
Ginger — 1 big piece
Garlic — 6 cloves
Onions — 2
Saffron — 1 tsp
Cardamoms — 8
Red chilli powder — 1 tsp
Green chillies — 4
Pepper — ½ tsp
Lime — 1
Clarified butter or oil — ½ cup
Mustard — ¼ tsp
Yogurt — ½ lb.
Coriander leaves — 1 bunch
Salt — to taste

Method

Flatten undercut pieces with kitchen hammer. Grind ginger, garlic, green chillies, coriander leaves and put on the meat. Slice onions fine and fry till brown. Strain excess oil. Heat saffron in a spoon over fire and grind saffron, fried onions and cardamoms together. Add to the meat. Add the remaining ingredients and mix well. Marinate for at least an hour. Cook in oil over low flame till tender.

Malpuray

Ingredients

Flour — 500 g
Eggs — 2
Milk — ½ glass
Water — ½ glass
Red pumpkin — 250 g

Method

Peel, boil and mash pumpkin. Beat all ingredients, including the mashed pumpkin together till a thin mixture is formed. Grease frying pan with oil and pour spoonfuls of batter into it till a thin, even layer [as for a pancake] is formed. When one side is done, turn it over. Put a little more oil on the sides of the *malpura* so that it fries properly and remove when done. Repeat the process till all the mixture is used up.

Palak Paneer

Ingredients

Fresh spinach — ½ kg
Onion — 1 large (chopped fine)
Garlic paste — 1 tsp
Ginger paste — 1 tsp
Coriander powder — ¼ tsp
Red chilli powder — ¼ tsp
Yogurt — ¼ cup
Oil — 2 tbsp
Tomatoes — 2 (chopped fine)
Cumin powder — ¼ tsp
Turmeric powder — ¼ tsp
Fenugreek leaves — ½ tsp (crushed)
Fresh cream — 8 oz
Cottage cheese — 1 pkt
Salt — to taste

Method

Boil spinach lightly; drain water; and mash with hand grinder. Heat oil in a wok, and sauté onions. Add tomatoes, ginger and garlic pastes and all the dry ingredients. Fry well, stirring constantly. Add spinach and stir-fry for two minutes till well-mixed. Add yogurt and simmer for two minutes. Cut cottage cheese into cubes and fry them till light brown. Add them in the spinach and cook. Add fresh cream and stir till the mixture thickens. Serve hot.

Burani

Ingredients

Eggplant — 1 large
Onions —2 large
Tomatoes — 2 large
Yogurt — ¼ kg
Garlic — 5–6 cloves
Oil — ⅛ cup
Crushed garlic — ½ tsp
Salt and pepper — to taste

Method

Soak eggplants; cut into thick rounds and fry till light brown. Fry onions till brown, and dice tomatoes. Blend onions, tomatoes, and garlic together. Fry the masala in oil and sprinkle salt and pepper on it. When masala is well *bhooned*, add eggplants. Mash and keep on *dum* for few minutes, constantly stirring. Remove from flame.

Beat yogurt with some salt and crushed garlic. Just before serving, place yogurt in a deep dish and pour the eggplant mixture in the centre.

Chicken Makhni (Butter chicken)

Ingredients

Chicken — 1 (cut-up in 8 pieces)
Yogurt — 1 cup
Cream — 1 cup
Garlic paste — 1 tsp
Butter — 3 oz
Tomato puree — 1 cup
Red chilli powder — 1 tsp (heaped)
Ginger paste — 1 tsp
Green chilli paste — 1 tsp
Red food colour — few drops
Salt — to taste

Method

Marinate chicken for at least three hours with ¼ cup yogurt, ginger, green chilli paste, red chilli powder, colour and salt. Heat butter and fry chicken for ten minutes till slightly brown. Add remaining yogurt and tomato puree. Cook on medium flame till chicken is tender. Add fresh cream and cook till gravy thickens. Give *dungar*.

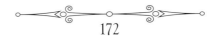

Dum Aloo

Ingredients

Potatoes — 1 kg (small, boiled and cut into halves)
Cumin — 3 tbsp (ground coarsely)
Coriander seeds — 3 tbsp (ground coarsely)
Red chillies (whole, long) — 1 tsp
Garlic — 1 bulb (ground)
Tamarind — 50 g
Curry leaves — few
Oil — ½ cup
Salt— to taste

Method

Soak the red chillies in water and then grind them coarsely. (If all the masalas are ground the traditional way on *seel-batta* rather than in a grinder, it will enhance the flavour of the ingredients.) Soak tamarind in hot water and remove the seeds. Mix thoroughly all the dry and wet ingredients and coat potatoes with it. Heat oil. Drop curry leaves in it and let the oil smoke, then pour it over the potatoes. Cover it tightly so that the potatoes imbibe the aroma of the curry leaves.

Mince Cutlets

Ingredients

Mince meat — ¼ kg
Potatoes —3 large
Onions — 2 large
Coriander powder — 2 tsp
Red chilli powder — ½ tsp
Ginger — 1 tsp
Garlic — 1 tsp
Vermicelli — as required
Egg — 1
Oil — for frying
Coriander leaves, mint leaves and green chillies — 1 tbsp (chopped)
Salt — 1 tsp

Method

Boil potatoes. Slice one onion finely, and chop the other. Fry the sliced onion in little oil till light brown. Add ginger and garlic, mince, coriander powder, chilli powder and salt. Cook until the water dries up, *bhoonno*, and remove from fire. Mash potatoes and mix with the mince. Fry the chopped onion lightly and add to the mince. Beat egg. Make balls from the mince and potato mixture. Dip in egg and then coat with crushed vermicelli, and deep fry.

Shahi Tukray

Ingredients

Bread — 6 slices
Milk — 1½ kg
Sugar — 1¾ cups
Cardamoms — 3 or 4
Almonds — handful
Cashew nuts — handful

Method

Fry slices of bread until golden-brown. Boil milk until it thickens. Add sugar (milk should taste a little sweeter than normal). Boil cashews and almonds. Peel and slice them and add to the thickening milk while stirring constantly. When the quantity of milk is reduced to half, immerse the bread slices in the milk and cook on low heat. Do not stir. Crush cardamoms and sprinkle over the slices. When the slices are so soaked that they begin to break when lifted, take them out carefully one by one and lay them on the bottom of a shallow serving dish. Continue heating the milk till it thickens further, and pour over the bread slices. Serve at room temperature or warm.

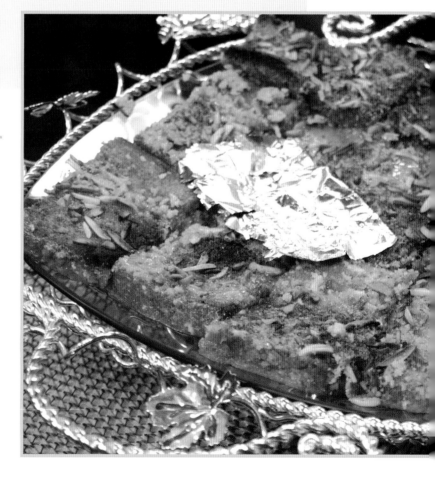

14

Recipes from Across Pakistan

Darbesh (Pashtun)

Ingredients

Semolina — 4 cups
Clarified butter — 1½ cups
Jaggery — 2 cups (crushed)
Dry fruits — as required

Method

Boil some water and add jaggery to make syrup. Heat clarified butter and fry semolina in it until golden. Add jaggery syrup and cook until dry. Add dry fruits of choice and mix well. Layer a tray with this mixture. Use a rolling pin to flatten and even out the surface, and leave to set. Cut into small squares and serve.

Bannu Kebab (Bannuchi)

Ingredients

Boneless sirloin of lamb —1 kg (cut, cleaned and cubed)
Garlic paste — 1 tsp
Ginger paste — 1 tsp
Green chilli paste — 1 tsp
Pepper — 1 tsp (ground coarsely)
Cardamom powder — ½ tsp
Eggs — 2 (beaten)
Raw papaya paste — 2 tbsp
Salt — to taste
Butter or oil — enough to brush

Method

Mix garlic, ginger and chilli paste together and rub on meat along with cardamom powder and salt. Set aside for a few hours. Coat meat cubes with beaten eggs. Sprinkle pepper. Either charcoal-grill (*sigri*) the meat on skewers, or roast in a pre-heated oven for about 10 minutes, brushing it regularly with butter/oil. Allow excess moisture to drain. Serve hot with *roomali roti*.

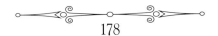

Boli (Hindkowan)

Ingredients

Buffalo milk — 1 kg (milk should be extracted third day after the buffalo has given birth)
Ground cardamom — ½ tsp
Almonds — ¼ kg (slivered)
Sugar — to taste

Method

Boil milk and add the rest of the ingredients. Keep stirring till mixture thickens into custard. Cool and serve.

Kabuli Pulao (Afghani)

Ingredients

Basmati (long-grained) rice — 2 cups
Moong beans — ½ cup (split, skinless)
Chicken breast— 1 lb. (boneless, cut into
    small cubes)
Clarified butter — ½ cup
Onions — ¾ cup (chopped)
Ginger — 1 inch piece (chopped)
Cinnamon — 2 sticks (broken in half)
Black peppercorns — 6
Cumin seeds — ½ tsp
Black cardamoms — 3 (cracked open)
Cloves — 6
Almonds — 2 tbsp
Raisins — 2 tbsp
Chicken broth —5 cups
Water — 4 cups
Salt — ¾ tsp

Method

Wash and soak rice and *moong* beans for 30 minutes. Drain and set aside. Heat clarified butter in a heavy-bottom pan. Add cumin seeds. Sauté for 2 minutes till seeds start to turn brown. Add onions and sauté till golden-brown. Add ginger and sauté some more. Add chicken, cinnamon, peppercorns, cardamoms, cloves and salt. Sauté till chicken begins to turn white. Add rice and *moong* beans, and stir well. Add water, almonds, raisins, and chicken stock. Bring to a boil. Lower heat and cook covered till done (approximately 20 minutes).

Pocha (Balti)

Ingredients

Water — 6 cups

Salt — ¼ tsp

Milk — ½ cup

Tea leaves — 1 tbsp

Butter — 2 tbsp

Method

Boil water and add tea leaves. Cook till it achieves a dark brown colour. Strain tea leaves from water and blend. Add salt, butter and milk and blend again for 2 or 3 minutes. Serve immediately.

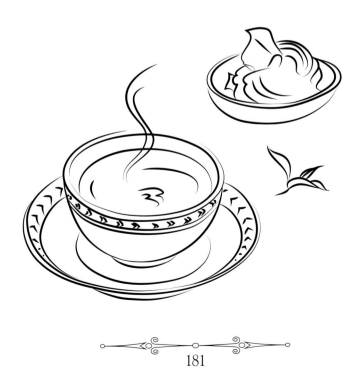

Girgir Aloo (Hunzakutz)

Ingredients

Pink split lentils — 2 cups
Oil — ¼ cup
Onions — 3 large (diced)
Tomatoes — 4 (ripe)
Cilantro/coriander — 1 (small bunch chopped)
Potatoes — 12 (small)
Green chillies (fresh) — 4
Sweet paprika — 2 tsp
Paprika or cayenne pepper — 2 tsp
Turmeric — 1 tsp
Salt — 1 tsp

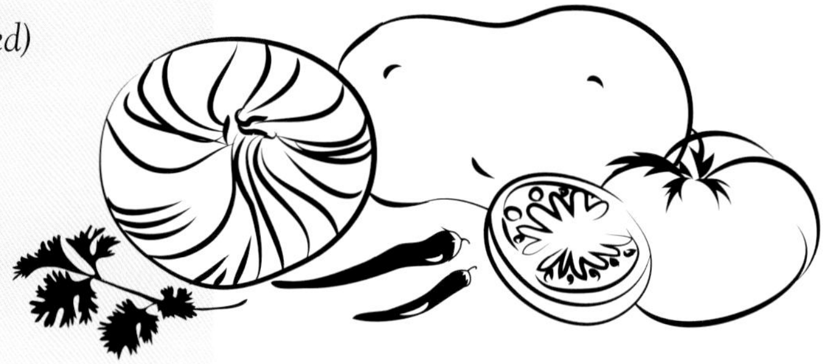

Method

Cook lentils in 2 cups water with ½ tsp salt, until tender. Heat oil in a large saucepan. Add onions and cook on low heat till golden-brown. Scald tomatoes in boiling water; remove skin and seeds, and cut into pieces. Add tomatoes and half of the cilantro in saucepan. Cook for a few minutes and add potatoes, chillies and spices. Stir and cook for a while, then add a cup of water. Cook until potatoes are done, and add lentils along with remaining water, if any. Stir and continue to cook for another 20 minutes. Before serving, stir in the remaining cilantro leaves.

Gushtaba (Kashmiri)

Ingredients

Boneless meat (leg of lamb) — 1 kg
Mustard oil —1 cup
Curd — 1 cup
Green cardamom — 5 pods
Cloves — 2
Cinnamon — 1 large stick
Fennel powder — 3 tsp
Asafoetida — 1 tsp

Meat fat — 1 cup
Milk — 2 cups
Water — 6 cups
Bay leaves — 2
Large cardamom — 3 (powdered)
Ginger powder — 1 tsp
Dried mint — 2 tsp
Salt — to taste

Method

Traditionally the meat is pounded with a wooden mallet on a smooth stone, although a grinder could be used for the purpose. Add the meat fat (a good substitute could be egg-white) and pound it well. Add cardamom powder, ginger powder and salt; keep pounding till it becomes a smooth pulp. Make round balls 2 to 3 inches in diameter and leave aside. Make sure they don't stick to one another. Heat oil in a large vessel. Put a little salt and asafoetida in it. Beat curd; add to the oil and keep stirring till it mixes well. Mix water; remaining whole and powdered spices; and milk together, and add in the oil. Bring the gravy to boil. Add meat balls one by one to the boiling gravy. Cook for one hour on medium flame, and simmer for about 15 minutes. Sprinkle with mint and serve with boiled rice.

Mutton Qorma (Mughlai)

Ingredients

Mutton — 500 g (cut into pieces)
Yogurt — 1 cup
Red chilli powder — 2 tsp
Coriander powder — 1 tsp
Turmeric powder — ¼ tsp
Mixed spices powder — 1 tsp
Tomato puree — 2 tbsp
Ginger/garlic — 1 tsp
Salt — 1 tsp

Oil — ¼ cup
Onions — 2 (diced)
Black peppercorns — 2
Green cardamom — 1
Cinnamon — 1 stick
Cloves — 2
Almonds ground — 2 tbsp
Screwpine — few drops

Method

Heat oil and fry onions till golden-brown. Remove and crush them, and set aside. In the same oil add whole spices along with mutton, ginger/garlic and salt. Stir and cook for approximately 8 to 10 minutes or till water evaporates and oil separates. Whip yogurt with red chillies, coriander, turmeric, mixed spices powder and tomato puree and add the mixture to the meat. Fry until oil separates. Mix the crushed onions with almonds and add to meat. Cook till meat is tender. Sprinkle screwpine and serve.

Sambusa (Tajik)

Ingredients

Flour — 4 cups
Eggs — 2
Water —1 cup
Vegetable Oil — 3 tsp
Mutton — 500 g
Onions — 2 medium (chopped)
Ginger paste — ½ tsp
Garlic paste — ½ tsp
Red chilli powder — ½ tsp
Salt — to taste

Method

Mince mutton. Heat oil in a pan and add onions. Sauté for a while and add ginger, garlic, salt and red chillies. Add mutton and fry till cooked. In a bowl mix flour, eggs, salt and water and prepare dough out of it. Leave for 30–40 minutes. Make small balls out of the dough. Roll each ball flat and put a spoonful of filling in the middle and fold into a triangle. Bake the triangles in an oven until the outer covering changes its colour.

Buuz (Mongol)

Ingredients

For dough:

All-purpose flour — 2 cups   Water — ¾ cup (hot)

Salt — a pinch

Mix hot water and flour and knead to form smooth, soft dough. Wrap in plastic and chill in the refrigerator for one hour.

Buuz dipping sauce:

Soya sauce — ¼ cup   Vinegar — ¼ cup

Chilli oil — 1 tsp   Ginger root — 1 tbsp (finely grated)

Combine all ingredients in a jar with a tight-fitting lid; shake vigorously and let stand for one hour for the flavours to blend.

For filling:

Ground lamb or beef — ½ lb   Onion — ½ (finely chopped)

Garlic — 3 cloves (finely crushed)   Ginger root —1 tbsp (finely crushed)

Curry powder — 2 tsp   Flour — 2 tsp

Soya sauce — 2 tsp   Chilli paste — ½ tsp

Combine all ingredients in a large bowl. Mix thoroughly and keep aside.

Method

Divide the dough into walnut-size balls. On a floured board, roll each ball into a thin flat circle — about 2 inches in diameter. Alternately, a cookie cutter or a glass could be used. Place a tablespoon of the filling in the centre of each circle of dough. Dumplings may be formed in two styles. For a half-moon shape, fold the dough in half over the filling and pinch the edges to seal. For a sachet-style dumpling, pinch the dough into a series of tiny pleats, gathering the edge together into a tightly puckered rosette at the top.

Place dumplings in a bamboo steamer and steam over boiling water for 30 minutes till glossiness appears. Remove dumplings from steamer and serve immediately with dipping sauce.

Chickpea Curry (Khowistani)

Ingredients

Chickpeas — 850 gms (boiled and not drained)
Coriander/cilantro – 1 bunch
Green jalapenos — 2 small
Mixed spices — 2 tbs
Garlic — 4 cloves (sliced)
Butter — 2 tbsp
Canola oil — 2 tbsp

Method

Heat butter and oil over medium heat. Add garlic, stirring vigorously to prevent browning. Cut jalapenos in half; remove seeds. Add chickpeas and jalapenos and cook over low flame. Stir continuously to prevent burning. Add mixed spices after 10 minutes and continue to stir until ingredients are combined and gravy thickens. Garnish with chopped coriander.

Paya (Punjabi)

Ingredients

Mutton trotters — 6
Salt — 2 tsp (heaped)
Black peppercorns — 4
Cloves — 4
Water — 8–10 cups
Oil — ½ cup
Chilli powder — 2 tsp (heaped)
Yogurt (beaten) — ¼ kg
Mixed spice powder — 1 tsp

Ginger/garlic — 1 tsp
Turmeric — 1 tsp
Green cardamoms — 4
Bay leaf — 1
Cinnamon — 1 piece
Onions — 2 (fried brown and crushed)
Coriander powder — 2 tsp (heaped)
Tomato paste — ½ cup

Method

Cook cleaned trotters with 1 tsp ginger/garlic, salt, turmeric, peppercorns cardamoms, cloves, bay leaf and cinnamon in water till tender, keeping flame low for 2–3 hours. Save 2–3 cups stock. Heat oil and add ginger/garlic. Fry for 5 minutes. Add chilli powder, coriander powder, the left-over stock and trotters, and fry. Add yogurt mixed with crushed onions and tomato paste. Cook for 5–10 minutes. Add enough water for 2 cups gravy to remain and let it cook on low heat for 15 minutes. Remove from fire. Sprinkle mixed spice powder and serve with sliced ginger, lemon, coriander leaves and *naan*.

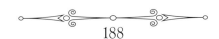

Khara Prashad (Sikh)

Ingredients

Clarified butter — 1 cup, or unsalted butter ½ lb.
Whole-wheat flour — 1 cup
Sugar — 1 cup
Water — 3 cups

Method

Boil sugar and water to make light syrup. Meanwhile, melt clarified butter or unsalted butter in a pan. Add whole-wheat flour to it and stir mixture continuously, till butter separates and the flour turns a deep golden. Add boiling sugar syrup to the mixture. Stir rapidly until all water is absorbed. Keep stirring until the mixture thickens into a firm pudding. When ready, the *prashad* slides easily from the pan into a serving bowl.

Sajji (Baloch)

Ingredients

Lamb full — 8 kg
Vinegar — 2 tbsp
Salt — 3 tbsp
Lemon juice — ½ cup
Papaya (raw, peeled and crushed) — 500 g

Method

Mix ingredients together to make a paste and rub them evenly on the lamb. Leave it overnight or for at least 6 hours in the fridge. Grill the lamb on charcoal till tender and serve.

Mantu (Hazara)

Ingredients

Bread — 6 slices	Milk — 1½ kg
Sugar — 1¾ cups	Cardamoms — 3 or 4
Almonds — handful	Cashew nuts — handful
Minced lamb — 1 kg	Onion — 1 large (finely chopped)
Garlic — 2 to 4 cloves (grated or crushed)	Red chillies — 2 (finely chopped)
Black pepper — 1 tsp (freshly ground)	Coriander powder — 1 tbsp
Yogurt (plain) — 500 g	Fresh mint (for garnish) — 1 bunch
Oil — 3 tsp	Salt — to taste

For Wanton Wrappers:

Bread — 6 slices	Milk — 1½ kg
Sugar — 1¾ cups	Cardamoms — 3 or 4
Almonds — handful	Cashew nuts — handful
Plain flour — 2 cups	Water — ¾ cup

Method

Heat cooking oil in a frying pan. Add onions and fry until translucent. Add 2 cloves of garlic and meat and mix thoroughly. Cook until the meat is brown. Add seasonings, coriander and chillies, and continue to cook for 20 minutes adding only enough water, if at all, to prevent the meat from sticking. Allow the meat mixture to cool a little.

Mix the wrapper ingredients to make dough. Roll out the dough into circles. In between each dough-wrapper circle, place a teaspoon of meat mixture in the centre. Fold the wrapper to create a dumpling by lifting opposite corners and sealing them together with wet fingers. Repeat with the remaining wrappers till all the filling is used up. Place the *mantu* in a steamer, and cook for 30 minutes. Create a sauce by mixing yogurt and remaining garlic together. To serve, cover the base of a large platter with yogurt sauce; place the *mantu* on it, piling them on top of one another to create a mound. Garnish by pouring a little sauce over the lot, then sprinkle some minced lamb, topped with mint leaves.

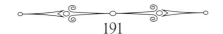

Thadal (Sindhi)

Ingredients

Water — 1½ litre
Sugar — 300 g
Milk — 250 ml.
Almonds — 20 pieces
Cantaloupe seeds — 1 tsp
Watermelon — 1 tsp
Aniseed — ½ *tbsp*
Cardamom powder — ½ *tbsp*
Poppy seeds — ½ *tbsp*
Black peppercorns — 10
Rosewater — 50 g

Method

Soak sugar in half litre water. Soak remaining dry ingredients in 400 ml. water and keep aside for 2–3 hours. Grind to a paste. Add remaining water and stir vigorously. Sieve the mixture; add sugar solution, milk and rose water. Mix well. Chill before serving.

Chicken Chow Mein (Chinese)

Ingredients

Ginger — 1 tbsp (fresh, grated)
Garlic cloves — 2
Tomato ketchup — 3 tbsp
Oyster sauce — 2 tbsp
Soya sauce (low salt) — 2 tbsp
Red capsicum — 1 large
Spring onions — 5
Bean sprouts — 200 g
Chicken breast — 1 large
Egg noodles — 3 nests
Sunflower oil — 1 tbsp

Method

Put ginger in a bowl; crush in the garlic, and add ketchup, oyster sauce, soya sauce and 3 tbsp water. Stir and keep aside. Cut red capsicum and spring onions into strips. Cut chicken into bite-size pieces. Boil noodles. Heat oil in wok and fry chicken till it changes colour. Add capsicum and stir-fry for 1 minute. Pour sauce into wok and stir well until bubbling. Add noodles, bean sprouts and spring onions a handful at a time and stir till well coated in sauce, and vegetables are tender.

Mulligatawny Soup (Anglo-Indian)

Ingredients

Butter —2 tbsp
Green chilli — 1 (seeded)
Red lentils — ¼ cup
Curry powder — 1 tbsp
Lemon — 1
Chicken — ½ –1 cup (boiled, shredded)

Onion — 1 large (peeled and chopped)
Chicken stock — 4 cups
Salt and pepper — to taste
Coconut milk — ½ cup
Rice — 1–2 cups (cooked)

For garnish — Some cream, lemon wedges

Method

Sauté onion in butter on low heat until onion turns translucent. Stir in curry powder, salt and pepper and cook for a minute. Pour in the stock; add the lentils and bring to a boil. Reduce heat and simmer for 30 minutes. When the soup is done; puree in a blender. Return to pot. Simmer again and add coconut milk and lemon juice. Serve in individual bowls by first putting in a spoon of rice at the bottom of the bowls, then a spoon of chicken and finally the soup. Garnish by swirling cream in the centre of the bowl. Serve with lemon wedges.

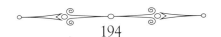

Kul kul (Goan)

Ingredients

All-purpose flour — 3½ cups
Baking powder — ½ tsp
Butter (un-salted) —1 tbsp
Eggs — 2 large (lightly beaten)
Coconut milk — 1 cup
Sugar — ¼ cup (powdered)
Vegetable oil — for frying

For glazing:
Sugar — 1 cup (granulated)
Water — ¼ cup

Method

Sieve flour and baking powder together. Set aside. Beat butter in a mixing bowl till soft. Add eggs, coconut milk and powdered sugar. Beat to make smooth mixture. Add flour. Knead to make soft dough and make small balls out of it. Flatten them on the back of a greased fork and roll them up to form cylinders. Deep fry on medium heat till the *kul kuls* start to turn golden brown. Remove on paper towel. Heat granulated sugar and water in a heavy-bottom pan till sugar is completely dissolved. When *Kul kuls* have cooled to room temperature, dip them in the syrup. Toss *Kul kuls* around so they are fully coated. Store in air tight container.

Nihari (Dilliwallay)

Ingredients

Beef (bong) — 1 kg
Nihari masala* — 4 tbsp
Ginger/garlic paste — 2 tbsp
Red chilli powder — 1 tbsp
Refined flour — 4 tbsp
Coriander powder — 1 tbsp
Clarified butter — 1 cup

Bone marrow — 1
Onions — ½ cup (chopped)
Salt — 1 tbsp
Wheat flour — 4 tbsp
Water — ½ cup + 10 cups
Yogurt — ½ cup

For Garnish

Coriander leaves — as required
Lemon — as required (finely sliced)

Green chillies — as required
Ginger — as required (finely sliced)

*Note: To make nihari masala, blend 2 tbsp fennel seeds, 3 cinnamon sticks, 6 green cardamoms, 2 black cardamoms, 15 peppercorns, 1 tbsp dried ginger, 6 pieces mace, less than half-a-piece of nutmeg, 1½ tbsp red chillies, ½ tsp turmeric powder and 1 tbsp coriander powder together in a blender.

Method

Heat clarified butter in a pot and fry onions till brown. Add ginger and garlic; fry and then add meat cut into large pieces, and bone marrow. Add salt, red chillies, nihari masala, yogurt and ½ cup water. Fry well. Add 10 glasses of water and simmer on low heat for 4 hours. Combine wheat and refined flour in a bowl; add water to make a thick mixture. Pass it through a strainer and gradually add to *nihari* pot, while continuously stirring till it acquires a thickish consistency. Add only as much mixture as required for the purpose. Cover the pot with a lid and leave to cook on low flame. Keep stirring from time to time so that the curry does not stick to the base. Dish out when oil appears on the surface. Garnish with coriander leaves, lemon, ginger and green chillies before serving.

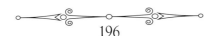

Seyal Phulka (Hindu)

Ingredients

Chapatis — 4 (at least one meal stale)
Green chillies — 2 (chopped)
Tomatoes —2 small (blended)
Curry leaves — few
Mustard seeds — ½ tsp
Garlic — 4 cloves
Turmeric powder — ¼ tsp
Coriander powder — 1 tsp
Coriander leaves — ½ bunch
Oil — 1 tsp
Water — 1½ cups
Lemon — 1
Salt — to taste

Method

Heat oil in a pan. Add chopped garlic and sauté till it changes colour. Add curry leaves and mustard seeds and let the seeds sputter. Add tomatoes, chillies, salt, turmeric and coriander powder and fry on high heat till tomatoes change colour. Add water. As soon as the mixture starts bubbling, break the *chapatis* into bite size pieces, and add to the boiling mixture. If the *chapatis* are stiff, you may require more water. Add half the coriander leaves and cook on *dum* till the water evaporates. Garnish with remaining coriander and a drizzle of freshly squeezed lemon juice.

Bagharay Baingan (Hyderabadi)

Ingredients

Eggplants — 500 g
Ginger — 5 g
Coriander seeds — 12 g
Peanuts — 70 g
Poppy seeds — 3 g
Fenugreek seeds — 2 g
Red chilli powder — 5 g
Tamarind — 75 g
Salt — to taste

Onions — 4 (medium)
Garlic — 2 cloves
Sesame seeds — 40 g
Cumin seeds — 5 g
Coconut — 20 g (desiccated)
Turmeric powder — 2 g
Jaggery — 6 g
Curry leaves — 4 g
Oil — 120 ml.

Method

Soak the tamarind in 1 cup water. Mash, and strain to extract tamarind water. Discard the residue and set aside. Wash the eggplants; make 2-inch slits along the length ensuring that the ends are intact. Roast the onions on a griddle till they soften and turn light golden brown.

Roast together on medium heat coriander seeds, sesame seeds, peanuts, cumin seeds, poppy seeds, desiccated coconut and the fenugreek seeds till they darken slightly and start emitting an aroma. Grind together the onions, roasted spices, ginger, garlic, salt, turmeric powder, red chilli powder and jaggery to a fine paste. Mix in the tamarind water. Keep aside some of this mixture and stuff the eggplants with the remaining mixture.

Heat oil, add curry leaves and sauté for a few minutes. Add the stuffed eggplants and fry for about 10 minutes. Add the reserved paste and mix gently. Add little water, cover and cook on medium heat, stirring occasionally but very gently. Cook till the eggplants are tender and oil leaves the sides of the pan. Serve hot.

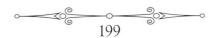

Bihari Kebab (Bihari)

Ingredients

Beef (raan, cut against the fibre into long thick strips) — 1 kg
Ginger — 2 inch piece (paste)
Salt — to taste
Mustard oil — 4 tbsp
Onions — 3 medium
Papaya (raw) — 3 inch piece (ground)
Cloves — 2
Cinnamon — 1 stick
Almonds — 6-8 (blanched without skin)
Poppy seeds (optional) — 1 tbsp
Yogurt — 4 tbsp
Black pepper — 1 tsp (powdered)
Red chilli powder — 1 tsp

Method

Marinate beef with ginger paste, salt and 2 tbsp oil for half to one hour. Grind cinnamon, cloves and almonds. Grind 2 onions and raw papaya together. Fry 1 onion golden brown. If using poppy seeds, wash them thoroughly and strain the water, then grind, preferably on a mortar. Mix all ingredients and marinate beef for two to three hours. Skewer the meat in a zig-zag manner so that it doesn't come off while barbecuing. Grill over charcoal. Brush with butter when the meat begins to turn golden.

Galavat Kebab (Luknawi)

Ingredients

Minced mutton — 500 g
Cashew paste — 25 g
Mixed spice powder (nutmeg, mace,
    cardamom, cloves, cinnamon) — 1 tsp
Ginger paste — 1 tbsp
Coriander powder — 1 tsp
Turmeric powder — 1 pinch
Yogurt — 1 cup
Oil — as needed

Poppy seed paste — 25 g
Papaya (raw) —100 g (paste)

Garlic paste — 1 tbsp
Onion paste — 2 tbsp
Cumin powder — 1 tsp
Black pepper powder — 2 tsp
Flour — 1-2 tbsp
Salt — to taste

Method

Marinate mutton with all ingredients other than flour and oil for minimum 1 hour (marinating it overnight is better). Add flour if the mixture is watery so that if you take some part of the mixture in your hands, it sticks together. Heat oil in a flat pan (*tawa*). Take small portions of the mixture; flatten it by hand and fry on low heat. Serve with onion rings and lemon.

Thepla (Gujarati)

Ingredients

Jaggery — 8 oz
Water — ½ cup
Wheat flour — 1 cup
Clarified butter — 2 tbsp (melted)
Oil — for frying

Method

Blend jaggery and water and add to wheat flour. Add clarified butter and mix into dough. Add water if necessary to get kneading consistency. Roll out into small rounds and deep fry. Take out on paper towels.

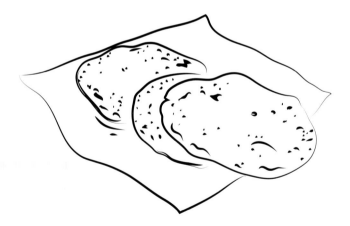

Bombay Biryani (Khoja)

Ingredients

Mutton or chicken — 1 kg (washed/cleaned, cut into pieces)

Rice (basmati) — 1 kg (soaked for 15 minutes)

Potatoes — 4 (steamed lightly, peeled and cut into large pieces)

Tomatoes — 6 (quartered)

Onions — 4 (medium, finely sliced)

Bay leaves — a few

Green chillies — 6 (whole)

Ginger/garlic paste — 1½ tbsp

Dried plums — 1 cup (soaked in hot water)

Red chillies — 1 tbsp (powdered)

Coriander powder — 2 tbsp

Peppercorns — 6

Cloves — 4

Cardamoms — 6

Black cumin seeds — 1 tsp

Yellow food colour — ¼ tsp

Yogurt — 1 cup

Milk — 1 cup (hot)

Clarified butter — 1 cup

Saffron — pinch (mixed in the hot milk)

Salt — to taste

Method

Mix yogurt, ginger/garlic, red chilli powder, 4 green chillies, coriander, some bay leaves, juice of 2 lemons, plums and salt in mutton or chicken. Mix thoroughly and set aside for half an hour.

Heat oil in a pan and fry onions till golden brown. Remove half of them on absorbent kitchen paper. In the remaining half add meat with yogurt and spices. Cook on low heat without adding water; when liquid evaporates, fry a little and remove from heat. Deep fry potatoes and separately fry tomatoes in a little oil. Add both tomatoes and potatoes to meat. Boil rice with remaining bay leaves, green chillies, cardamoms, black pepper, cloves and salt. Parboil rice and drain off water. Put a little oil in the base of pan and make a layer of half the rice. Then put a layer of the prepared meat and cover with a second layer of rice. Sprinkle saffron-infused milk over the rice and tightly seal pot. Keep on *dum* till rice is cooked. Serve with *raita* or *cachumer*.

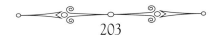

Dhokri (Memon)

Ingredients

Fish — ½ kg (cut into thick pieces)
Yogurt — ½ kg
Eggplant — 1 (cut into cubes)
Carrot — 1 (cut into cubes)
Green chillies — 4 (sliced)
Red chilli powder — 2 tsp
Turmeric powder — ½ tsp
Coriander powder — 2 tsp
Ginger/garlic paste — 1 tbsp

Onion — 1
Tamarind pulp — ½ cup
Potato — 1 (cut into cubes)
Peas — 1 cup
Coriander leaves — ½ bunch (chopped)
Mixed spices powder —½ tsp
Cumin seeds — 1 tsp
Oil — ½ cup and some more for frying
Salt — 1 tsp

For fritters:
Millet flour — 1 cup
Cumin seeds — ½ tsp
Water — as required

Salt — ½ tsp
Red chilli powder — 1 tsp

Method

Cut vegetables into thick pieces. Heat oil and fry onions till golden-brown. Add ginger and garlic paste and fry some more. Mix together yogurt, red chilli powder, cumin seeds, salt, turmeric powder, mixed spice powder and coriander powder. Add to onions. Add all vegetables and fry well. Add four glasses of water and cook.

To make fritters, mix all ingredients and knead into dough. Roll a little dough in your palm and shape into a fist. When the water in the vegetables comes to a boil, add the fritters and cook on *dum*. Rub little salt on fish and fry in little oil. When gravy thickens, add fish, green chillies, coriander leaves and tamarind pulp. Cook some more.

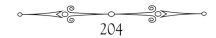

Haleem (Bohra)

Ingredients

Lamb — 1 kg
Cracked wheat — 500 g
Water — 3 litres
Salt — 3 tsp
Green masala paste
    (ginger, garlic and green chillies) — 3½ tsp
Onion — 1 (chopped)
Garnish — Sliced onions (fried brown),
    mint and julienned ginger, mixed spices powder

Method

Heat cracked wheat with 2 tsp *green masala* and 2 tsp salt in 2½ litres water. Make sure the pot is tightly sealed and covered with a heavy lid. When it comes to a boil, reduce heat and cook for approximately three hours. When the wheat is thoroughly cooked, mash with a hand blender. In a separate pot cook meat in ½ litre water, 1 tsp salt, 1½ tsp green masala, and chopped onion till meat is tender. De-bone meat and shred it. Add the meat mixture in the cooked wheat and mix thoroughly. Mash the ingredients and simmer till the flavours are well-infused and the *haleem* is of the required consistency (it should be like a thick paste). Take out in a serving dish and sprinkle mixed spice powder, mint, ginger and brown onions over it. Heat oil and give *baghar* just before serving.

Dhansak (Parsi)

Ingredients

Gram lentils — 50 g
Yellow lentils — 50 g
Mutton — 500 g (cubed)
Eggplant — 1 small (chopped)
Carrot — 1 (chopped)
Fenugreek — 1 bunch (chopped)
Oil — 4 tbsp

Pink lentils — 50 g
Split moong lentils — 50 g
Red pumpkin — 50 g (chopped)
White pumpkin — 50 g (chopped)
Onions — 1 (chopped)
Onions — 2 (sliced)

Masala ingredients:

Red dry chillies — 8
Coriander seeds — ½ tsp (roasted)
Cloves — 6
Ginger — 1 inch piece
Sambhar powder — 1 tbsp
Tomatoes — 2 large (chopped)
Jaggery — 1 tbsp

Cumin seeds — ½ tsp (roasted)
Cinnamon — ½ inch piece
Peppercorns — 6
Garlic — 8 cloves
Turmeric powder — ½ tsp
Coriander leaves — 2 tbsp (chopped)
Salt — to taste

Method

Soak lentils in water for at least an hour. Mix together the lentils, mutton and chopped vegetables; add enough water to cover the ingredients and bring to a boil. Simmer until meat and lentils are tender. When cooked, separate the meat from the lentils. Grind masala ingredients. Heat oil; fry sliced onions till brown. Add ground masala and fry, stirring continuously till aroma is emitted. Add tomatoes, coriander leaves, jaggery and salt, and cook on low heat for a couple of minutes. Blend the lentils and add to the masala mixture. Cook on low flame, stirring continuously till it comes to a boil. Add meat and continue cooking till thick. Serve with brown rice.

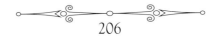

Meethi Dahi (Bengali)

Ingredients

Milk — 1 litre (full-cream)
Sugar — 200 g
Sweet curd — 2 tsp (if making in summer, use 3 tsp)

Method

Add 125 grams of sugar in milk and boil on high flame for 10 minutes. Heat remaining 75 grams of sugar in a heavy-bottom vessel with 2 tbsp water and melt on a low heat. Allow the mixture to become dark brown in colour. Gradually add this sugar mixture to the boiled milk and boil again for 5 minutes. Cool the mixture to lukewarm. Add the curd and mix well. Cover and allow the mixture to set for 6–8 hours and store in refrigerator.

Shawarma (Lebanese)

Ingredients

Chicken — 300 g (boneless, shredded)
Cucumber — as required (pickled)
Barbecue masala — 1 tbsp
Black pepper — ½ tsp (ground)
Lettuce leaves — as required (chopped)
Olives — as required
Tomatoes — as required
Pita bread — 6 to 8 pieces
Olive oil — 1 tbsp
Hummus, Garlic mayo sauce — as required
Salt — to taste

Method

Put 1 tbsp of olive oil in a pot; add the chicken and cook for 4–5 minutes. Add the barbecue masala, black pepper, salt and cook till the chicken is tender. Remove from heat. Split open pita bread. Place lettuce leaves, hummus, garlic mayo sauce, chicken, pickled cucumbers, olives and tomatoes on the bread and serve.

Khow Suey (Burmese)

Ingredients

Chicken or beef — 500 g (boneless, cubed)
Coriander powder — 2 tsp
Turmeric — ½ tsp
Garlic paste — 1 ½ tsp
Coconut milk powder — ½ cup
Oil — ½ cup
Salt — to taste

Tomato paste — 3 tbsp
Cumin powder – 2 tsp
Red chilli powder — 1 tsp
Ginger paste — 1 ½ tsp
Gram flour — 5 tbsp (roasted)
Spaghetti — 1 pkt. (boiled)

Method

Marinate meat with all ingredients except oil, spaghetti, coconut milk and gram flour. Heat oil and fry meat till golden-brown. Add coconut milk powder dissolved in 2 cups of water. Add three more cups of water and bring to boil. Mix gram flour with water to make a paste and strain through a strainer. Add to curry and cook till meat is tender. Serve with spaghetti, fried garlic, boiled and cut-up eggs, chopped onions, fried spaghetti, crushed red chillies, lemon, chopped green chillies and coriander.

Glossary

Urdu	English
A	
Aam	Mango
Aata	Whole-wheat flour
Achar	Pickle
Adrak	Ginger
Ajmoda	Parsley
Ajwain	Carom seeds
Akhrot	Walnut
Aloo	Potato
Aloo Gosht	Meat and potato curry
Aloobukhara	Dried plum
Amchoor	Dried mango powder
Amrood	Guavas
Anaar dana	Dried pomegranate seeds
Ananas	Pineapple
Angoor	Grapes
Arq gulab	Rosewater
Arvi	Colocasia/eddo
Asli/desi ghee	Clarified butterfat
B	
Badam	Almond
Badian	Star anise
Baghar/tarka	Tempering
Baingan	Eggplant
Bajra	Millet
Bajray ka aata	Millet flour
Bakray ka gosht	Mutton
Basmati rice	Long grain rice
Batair	Quail
Besan	Gram flour
Bhajia	Dumpling
Bhindi	Okra

Urdu	English
Bhoonna	Frying
Bhujia	Cooked vegetables
Bhuna chana	Roasted chickpeas
Bhutta/challi	Corn on the cob
Bund gobhi	Cabbage
C	
Chaaliya	Betel nut
Chaawal ka aata	Rice flour
Chanay ki daal	Gram daal, golden yellow lentils
Chandi ka varq	Sterling silver leaf (for garnish)
Charbi	Animal fat
Chasni	Sugar water
Chawal	Rice
Cheeni	Sugar
Chilka	Rind
Chini grass	China grass
Chowli daal	Split black-eyed peas
Chubars	Fruits
Chuqander	Beetroot
Curry patta	Curry leaves
D	
Daal	Split lentils/pulses
Dahi	Yogurt
Dahi ka paani	Whey
Dar cheeni	Cinnamon
Dastarkhwan	Floor dining-spread
Degchi/handi	Pot
Dhania	Coriander
Dhania patta	Coriander leaves/cilantro
Dhoan/dhungar	Smoking

Urdu	English
Doodh	Milk
Double roti	Bread
Double roti ka chura	Breadcrumbs
Dum pukht	Steaming

G

Urdu	English
Gaajar	Carrot
Gaiey ka gosht	Beef
Gandana	Leeks
Ganna	Sugarcane
Garam masala	Mixed spices (cardamoms, cloves, black pepper, cinnamon and nutmeg)
Gehon	Broken wheat/cracked wheat
Gehon ka aata	Whole-wheat flour
Ghee	Clarified butter
Gosht	Meat
Gowaar phalli	Cluster beans
Gulaab ka ark	Rose water
Gundh	Edible gum
Gundha hua aata	Dough
Gur	Jaggery
Gurday	Kidneys

H

Urdu	English
Haldi	Turmeric
Havan dasta	Pestle and mortar
Hara dhania	Coriander leaf
Hara lassan	Garlic chives
Hari mirch	Green chilli
Hari pyaaz	Spring onions
Heeng	Asafoetida

Urdu	English

I

Urdu	English
Ilaichi	Cardamom
Imli	Tamarind

J

Urdu	English
Jaifal	Nutmeg
Javithry	Mace
Jheenga	Prawns/shrimps
Joh	Barley
Jowar	Sorghum

K

Urdu	English
Kaaju	Cashew nut
Kaalay chanay	Black chickpeas/Bengal gram
Kaala zeera	Black cumin
Kabuli chanay	Chickpeas
Kaddu	Pumpkin
Kaila	Banana
Kairi	Green mango
Kala namak	Black salt
Kalaiji	Liver
Kali mirch	Black pepper
Kalmi shora	Saltpetre (potassium nitrate)
Kalonji	Nigella/onion seeds
Karaela	Bitter gourd
Karhai	Wok
Karhi patta	Curry leaves
Kasoori methi	Dry fenugreek leaves
Katchnar	Bauhinieae plant family
Kesar/zafran	Saffron
Kewra	Screwpine
Khajoor	Dates

Urdu	English	Urdu	English
Khameer	Yeast	*Meetha*	Dessert
Khar shaf	Artichoke	*Methi*	Fenugreek seeds
Kharbooza	Muskmelon/cantaloupe	*Mewa*	Dry fruits
Kheera	Cucumber	*Mirch*	Chilli
Khoya, mawa	Dried whole milk, thickened milk	*Mithai*	Sweetmeat
		Mogo	Cassava
Khubani	Apricot	*Mooli*	Radish
Khuskhus	Poppy seeds	*Moong ki daal*	Split moong beans
Kishmish	Raisins/currants	*Mung phali*	Peanuts
Kokum	Wet mangostein	*Murghi*	Chicken
Kondi	Dehydrated meat	*Murmure*	Puffed rice
Kuar gandhal	Aloe		

L

Laal mirch	Red chilli		

N

Urdu	English	Urdu	English
Laal mirch	Red chilli	*Namak*	Salt
Lassan	Garlic	*Narial*	Coconut
Lassi	Buttermilk	*Nashpati*	Pear
Lavang	Clove	*Neem*	Margosa
Lawki	Bottle gourd/vegetable marrow		
Limbu	Lime or lemon		
Lobia	Kidney beans		

P

Urdu	English	Urdu	English
		Paalak	Spinach

M

Urdu	English	Urdu	English
Maash ki daal	White lentil	*Paan*	Betel leaf
Machli	Fish	*Paani*	Water
Magaz	Brain	*Palla machli*	Elicia
Maida	Plain white flour	*Paneer*	Cottage cheese
Makai	Corn/maize	*Papeeta*	Papaya
Makai ka aata	Maize flour	*Paplait*	Pomfret
Makhan	Butter	*Pasanday*	Beef undercut
Malai	Whole cream	*Paya*	Trotters
Masoor ki daal	Pink lentils (split)	*Phali*	Green beans
Matar	Peas	*Phool gobhi*	Cauliflower
		Pista	Pistachio
		Pudina	Mint
		Pyaaz	Onion

Urdu	English
Q	
Qeema	Mince
R	
Rahu	Carp
Rai dana	Mustard seeds
S	
Saabit lal mirch	Whole red chilli
Saag	Mustard greens
Sabit moong	Whole green gram
Sabzi	Vegetables
Saib	Apple
Saim ki phali	Broad beans
Santra	Orange
Sarson ka tail	Mustard oil
Saunf	Aniseed/fennel seeds
Seekh	Skewer
Sewayian	Vermicelli
Shehed	Honey
Shakarkand	Sweet potato
Shaljam	Turnip
Sheera	Sugar syrup
Shimla mirch	Capsicum
Sigri	Charcoal grill
Sinda namak	Rock salt
Singhara	Water chestnuts
Sirqa	Vinegar
Siyah ilaichi	Black cardamom
Siyah zeera	Black cumin fruits
Sooji	Semolina
Sounth	Dry ginger
Soya	Dill
Subz piyaz	Spring onions

Urdu	English
Subzi	Vegetables
Sufaid chana	Chickpeas
T	
Tail	Oil
Tamatar	Tomato
Tandoor	Oven
Tarbooz	Watermelon
Tawa	Cast-iron griddle pan
Teetar	Partridge
Tej patta	Bay leaf
Thali	Steel platter
Til	Sesame seeds
Tinday	Baby pumpkin
Toor daal/arhar	Yellow lentils
Tukham-i-balanga/sabja/takmaria	Basil seed
Tulsi	Basil
Turai	Ribbed gourd or Ridge gourd
U	
Urad ki daal/maash ki daal	Black lentil
V	
Varq	Sterling silver leaves
Y	
Yakhni	Stock
Z	
Zardalu	Dried apricot
Zeera	Cumin (white)
Zetoon	Olives
Zetoon ka tail	Olive oil

Bibliography

- Agriculture Statistics, NWFP, Peshawar (2005–2006 to 2007–2008).

- Ali, Mubarak, 'Feast for a King', *Dawn*, Sunday Magazine, 23 March 2008.

- Aseer, Sher Wali Khan, 'Khow Culture: Unique Identity and Challenges', paper presented at the Seminar on Lawari Tunnel Project—Khow Culture: Views and Reviews–II, held by Chitral Development Organization, February 2009.

- Banerji, Chitrita, *Eating India: An Odyssey into the Food and Culture of the Land of Spices*, Bloomsbury, USA, 2007.

- Blood, Peter R. (ed.), *Pakistan: A Country Study*, Federal Research Division, Library of Congress, Area Handbook Series, 6th edition, 1995.

- Bruun, Ole, and Arne Kalland (eds.), *Asian Perceptions of Nature: A Critical Approach*, Nordic Institute of Asian Studies, Studies in Asian Topics, No. 18, Curzon Press, Surrey, 1995.

- Caroe, Olaf, *The Pathans: 550 B.C.–A.D. 1957, With a new epilogue*, Oxford University Press, Karachi, 1976.

- Chapman, Pat, *Curry Club: Balti Curry Cookbook*, Piatkus, United Kingdom, 1993.

- Chatterjee, Suhas, *Indian Civilization and Culture*, M.D. Publications Pvt. Ltd., New Delhi, 1998.

- Collingham, Lizzie, *Curry: A Tale of Cooks and Conquerors*, Vintage, 2006.

- Devendra, C.; Thomas, D.; Jabbar, M.A.; Zerbini, E., *Improvement of livestock production in crop-animal systems in the agro-ecological zones of South Asia*, International Livestock Research Institute, Nairobi (Kenya), 2000.

- Flowerday, Julie M., and Mareile Paley, 'Cooking in Hunza', Vol. 57, Issue 3, *Saudi Aramco World*, http://www.saudiaramcoworld.com/issue/200603/cooking.in.hunza.htm, 2006.

- Garg, Ganga Ram, *Encylopaedia of the Hindu World: Volume 1*, Concept Publishing Company Pvt. Ltd., New Delhi, 1992.

- Gidwani, Bhagwan S., *Return of the Aryans*, Penguin Books India, New Delhi, 2006.

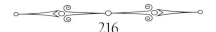

- Gupta, Om, *Encyclopaedia of India, Pakistan and Bangladesh*, Gyan Publishing House, New Delhi, 2006.

- Hoiberg, Dale and Indu Ramchandani (eds.), *Students' Britannica India, Volume 6: Select Essays*, Encyclopaedia Britannica (India), Popular Prakashan Pvt Ltd., India, 2000.

- Hughes-Buller, R., *Imperial Gazetteer of India: Provincial Series: Baluchistan*, Sang-e-Meel Publications, Lahore, 1991.

- Kalra, J. Inder Singh and Pradeep Das Gupta, *Prashad Cooking with Indian Masters*, Allied Publishers Pvt. Ltd., India, 1986; 25th reprint, 2005.

- Khan, Teepu Mahabat, *The Tribal Areas of Pakistan*, Sang-e-Meel Publications, Lahore, 2008.

- Kenoyer, Jonathan Mark, 'Measuring the Harappan World: Insights into the Indus Order and Cosmology', in *The Archaeology of Measurement: Comprehending Heaven, Earth and Time in Ancient Societies*, edited by Iain Morley and Colin Renfrew, Cambridge University Press, Cambridge, 2010.

- Lakda, Shamime, *Dhaal-Chaawal Palidu: A Collection of Bohra Recipes*, Book Art, 2002.

- Lari, Yasmeen, *Karachi Heritage Guide*, Heritage Foundation, Karachi, 2000.

- Latif, Abdul, *Population Census of Pakistan, 1972*, District Census Report, Volume 1, Census Organisation (Pakistan), Manager of Publications, Karachi, 1975.

- Lilani, Pinky, *Spice Magic—An Indian Culinary Adventure*, Development Dynamics, 2001.

- Meadows, Azra and P.S. Meadows (eds.), *Indus River—Biodiversity, Resources, Humankind*, Oxford University Press, Karachi, 1999.

- Miller, Frederic P.; Agnes F. Vandome; John Mcbrewster (eds.), *Hindkowans*, Alphascript Publishing, Mauritius, 2010.

- Minority Rights Group International, World Directory of Minorities and Indigenous Peoples—Pakistan: Pathans, available at: http://www.unhcr.org/refworld/docid/49749cd22.html, 2008.

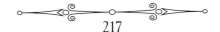

- Monier-Williams, Monier, *Modern India and the Indians*, first published in 1891, Kegan Paul, Trench, Trübner & Co Ltd; reprinted in 2000, Routledge, London, Great Britain.

- Nariman, Bapsi, *A Gourmet's Handbook of Parsi Cuisine*, Tarang Paperbacks, 1987.

- Nielson, Paula I., 'Who are the Pashtun People of Afghanistan?', http://paula-i-nielson.suite101.com/who-are-the-pashtun-people-of-afghanistan-a192535, 22 January 2010.

- Nijjar, B.S., *Origins and History of Jats and Other Allied Nomadic Tribes of India, 900 B.C.–1947 A.D.*, Atlantic Publishers & Distributors, 2007.

- Nyrop, Richard F. (ed.), *Pakistan—A Country Study*, 5th ed., Washington, DC, Secretary of the Army, 1984.

- Pant, Pushpesh and Huma Mohsin, *Food Path: Cuisine along the Grand Trunk Road from Kabul to Kolkata*, Roli Books, New Delhi, 2005.

- Papiha, Surinder Singh; Ranjan Deka; Ranajit Chakraborty, *Genomic Diversity: Application in Human Population Genetics*, Proceedings of a Symposium on Molecular Anthropology in the Twenty-First Century, held during the 14th International Congress of the Association of Anthropological and Ethnological Sciences, held 26 July–1 August 1998, in Williamsburg, Virginia, USA, Kluwer Academic/Plenum Publishers, New York, 1999.

- Poladi, Hassan, *The Hazaras*, Mughal Publishing Company, Stockton, California, 1989.

- Possehl, Gregory L., *The Indus Civilization: A Contemporary Perspective*, AltaMira Press, USA, 2002.

- Pruthi, R.K., *Indus Civilization*, Discovery Publishing House, New Delhi, 2004.

- Quddus, S.A., *The Tribal Baluchistan*, Ferozsons (Pvt.) Ltd., Lahore, 1990.

- Sen, Colleen Taylor, *Food Culture in India*, Greenwood Press, USA, 2004.

- Sener, Bilge (ed.), *Biodiversity: Biomolecular Aspects of Biodiversity and Innovative Utilization*, Proceedings of the 3rd IUPAC International Conference on Biodiversity (ICOB-3), 3–8 November 2001, Antalya, Turkey, Kluwer Academic/Plenum Publishers, New York, 2002.

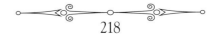

- Sharar, Abdul Halim, *Purana Lucknow* (*Guzishta Lucknow*), National Book Trust, New Delhi, 1971.
- Sharif, M. and B.K. Thapar, 'Food-producing communities in Pakistan and northern India', in *History of Civilizations of Central Asia, Volume I: The Dawn of Civilization: Earliest Times to 700 B.C.*, edited by Ahmad Hasan Dani and Vadim Mikhailovich Masson Masson, Multiple History Series, Unesco, 1992; Motilal Banarsidass Publ., 1999.
- Singh, Sarina; Lindsay Brown; Mark Elliott, Paul Harding; Abigail Hole, Patrick Horton, *Lonely Planet India*, Country Guide Series, Lonely Planet Publications, 13th Revised edition, 2009.
- Southworth, Franklin C., *Linguistic Archaeology of South Asia*, Routledge Curzon, London, 2005.
- West, Barbara A., *Encyclopedia of the Peoples of Asia and Oceania, Volume 1*, Infobase Publishing, New York, 2009.
- Yimene, Ababu Minda, *An African Indian Community in Hyderabad: Siddi Identity, Its Maintenance and Change*, Cuvillier Verlag Gottingen, Germany, 2004.

Websites

- Chitralnews.com.
- Dr Drummond in Beibei, http://drummondinbeibei.blogspot.com/
- Encyclopaedia Britannica Online.
- Outlook magazine, 11 January 2010 issue, http://www.outlookindia.com/content5115.asp
- PakistaniDefence.com
- Wikepedia.

Newspaper

- *Dawn*, Sunday Magazine—various 'Food for Thought' columns.

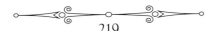

Index

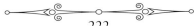

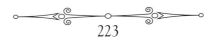

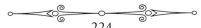

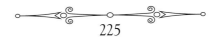

225

Mohajirs, 10, 110

Mohammed Bin Qasim, xiv

Mongol/Mongolian, xiv, 3, 5, 9, 43, 68, 72, 96, 186

Mughal, 5–7, 10, 17, 19, 31, 33, 39, 43, 48, 64, 68–71, 73–4, 76–7, 83, 95–6, 111, 115–17, 122–3, 125–6, 133, 135, 152, 154; Mughal dynasty, xiv; Mughlai specialties, 69

Mulberry, 4, 68

Mulligatawny soup, 128, 192

Multan, 7, 23, 27

Mumtaz Mahal, 70

Mustard, 5, 18, 29, 36, 43–4, 62, 74, 82–3, 85, 88, 116–7, 119, 120, 130, 135, 167, 183, 198, 200

Mutton qorma, 184

Muzaffarabad, 9, 74

N

Nadur yakhni, 78

Navroz, 61, 144, 159

Nawab Asaf-ud-Daula of Awadh, 18, 124

Nihari, 28, 85, 112, 196

Nimco, 151, 155

Nizams of Hyderabad, 44, 115

Nomads/nomadic, xiv, 3, 9, 19, 91, 93–5, 212

North Africa, 43

Nuts, 14, 26, 51, 59, 67, 72, 74, 77, 104, 107, 126, 159; almonds, 41, 58–9, 70–1, 79, 87, 89, 96, 102, 104, 114, 117–8, 123, 132–3, 140–1, 143, 145, 151, 175, 179, 180, 184, 191, 192, 200; cashews, 70, 75, 114, 127, 132, 136, 145, 151, 175, 191, 201; pistachio, 41, 59, 71, 79, 87, 89, 96, 115, 132, 133, 140–1, 143; walnuts, 4, 60, 62, 65, 74, 151

O

Oil/fat, 14, 16–8, 20, 26, 34, 36, 45, 51, 52, 54–5, 57–8, 61, 63–5, 72–3, 81, 116, 130, 142, 153, 183

Ovens, 206–7

P

Paan, 24, 46

Pakistan, xii–xv, 1–4, 6–7, 9, 11, 13, 15, 21, 23–25, 41, 43–4, 46, 56, 62, 64, 66, 67, 68, 69, 72, 76–7, 79, 88–9, 95, 99 105, 110, 111–12, 116, 119, 123, 127–30, 133, 136, 141, 146, 147, 151, 154, 157, 160

Pakistani Khoja cuisine, 133; specialties, 134

Pakoray, 89, 120, 142, 151, 158, 160

Palak paneer, 105, 126, 169

Parsis, 11, 110, 143–4, 159, 206

Pasanday, 167

Pashtun, 2–5, 6, 8, 10–1, 51–3, 55, 57–9, 62–3, 95, 102, 177; specialties, 53

Pashtu-speaking peoples of Balochistan, 9

Pastoral nomads, 9

Pastoral society, xiv

Paya, 28, 82–3, 126, 188

Persian, xiv–xv, 3, 6, 7, 9, 26, 43, 53, 59, 69, 70–2, 74, 76–8, 88, 95, 96, 111, 116–7, 144, 159

Peshawar, 4, 9, 23, 25–7, 51, 55

Pocha, 181

Poppy crop, 2

Portuguese, xiv, 44, 126–7, 129

Potatoes, 14, 26–8, 36, 44, 49, 52, 55, 61, 67, 69, 73, 75, 77, 83, 87, 99, 102, 106, 113, 120, 122–3, 131–2, 134–6, 138–9, 143–4, 151–4, 173–4, 182, 203–4

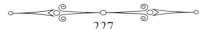